Trier
SAARLAND
Mainz
Mannheim
Main
Heidelberg
Bayreuth
Prague
Karlsruhe
Nuremberg
FRANCE
CZECHOSLOVAKIA
Baden-Baden
Stuttgart
Regensburg
FOREST
Ulm
Freiburg
Danube
Augsburg
BLACK
BAVARIA
Basel
Lake Constance
Munich
Konstanz
Lindau
Zürich
Oberammergau
Berne
Lucerne
Bregenz
Garmisch-Partenkirchen
Salzburg
Berchtesgaden
LIECHTENSTEIN
Interlaken
TYROL
Innsbruck
Kitzbühel
SWITZERLAND
AU
Davos
Bad Gastein
St Moritz
ITALY

CW01643225

Collins Phrase Books

German

Collins Phrase Books

FRENCH
GERMAN
ITALIAN
PORTUGUESE
SPANISH
SCANDINAVIAN
RUSSIAN
GREEK
YUGOSLAV
DUTCH

COLLINS PHRASE BOOKS

German

Compiled by

Edwin Carpenter
with
Marlies Pfeiffer

COLLINS
LONDON & GLASGOW

First Published 1981
Fourth Reprint 1984

Cover photographs
by courtesy of
Zefa London Ltd.
and Van Phillips

ISBN 0 00 433969 X

Printed in Great Britain
Collins Clear-Type Press

Contents

Contents

Introduction

For this Phrase Book, we hope we've thought of *almost* everything. If you can't speak German, the Collins German Phrase Book can help you say what you want whenever you want.

We've thought of what you'll be doing – driving and parking the car, having a drink in a café, buying stamps for your postcards. Each page has a clear heading so you can find your place quickly, and each section contains the phrases you are genuinely likely to need.

We've put ourselves in your shoes and tried to think of the situations that could catch you out. Have you ever wanted to ask which bus you ought to catch? or wished you knew the German for "disposable nappies"? These are just the kind of practical questions that you'll find here. And they are in simple but idiomatic German, with an easy-to-read pronunciation included.

Besides questions and phrases, we give you the information you need. Many sections begin with a few helpful tips on subjects like using the telephone or travelling by bus. There's a guide to food and wine, so you'll know what to try out, and a full set of conversion tables for everything from tyre pressures to shoe sizes. Bon voyage!

A Word of Advice

This book has been planned to make everything as easy to find as possible, but so that you won't have to fumble when you want a phrase in a hurry, try to read it through before you go away. There's no need to try and learn anything: just remember where the various sections come in the book. It will often be a good idea to look up a key word in the index, and this will take you to what you want to say.

How to Pronounce German

We've tried to make the pronunciation helps under the phrases as clear as possible. We've split words up to make them easy to read, but don't pause too long between the syllables. English spelling isn't enough to give a true idea of how German sounds, but if you listen to Germans talking and remember the points below, you'll find that German is not all that hard to pronounce and that you can read straight from the translations.

You'll notice some differences in the way the language is written. The most obvious of all is that all nouns begin with capital letters. There is also a letter which doesn't exist in English – ß – which is like *ss*.

Most letters are pronounced in much the same way as their English equivalents. However, when they appear at the end of a word *b* is pronounced like *p*, *d* like *t* and *g* like *k*; and *v* is pronounced like *f*, and *w* like *v*. Before *p* and *t* at the beginning of a word, and when it is combined with *ch*, *s* is pronounced like *sh* in *shock*.

The sign ¨ (the umlaut) often appears over German vowels, and makes a difference to the pronunciation – most of these are explained on the next page, but two sounds, *ö* and *ü*, are rather different from anything in English. We show *ö* as *ur'* because the nearest sound to it is in English words like *hurt*, but don't roll the *r*! The sound of *ü* can be made if you purse your lips and try to say *ee*.

We show the sound of the letters *ei* in two ways. It's common enough in English, the sound in *high* and *fine*, but English has at least ten ways of spelling it! We use either *ye* (*frei* = *frye*), or *i . . . e* when there is a consonant after it (*mein* = *mine*). In German, *e* has three sounds. We use a special symbol, *è*, for one of them, the weak sound it has in English *garden*.

Finally, don't be disconcerted by odd combinations of letters in the pronunciations, such as *shtrah-sè*. Just take it slowly and you'll be all right. And don't be confused by traditional English spellings – for example, *ow* means the sound in *cow* not the one in *low*, even in a word like *laufen* (***low***-*fèn*).

How to Pronounce German

German Spelling	Closest English Sound	Shown here by	Example	
a	cat	*a*	das	*dass*
	or father	*ah*	haben	***hah**-bèn*
ä	met	*e*	Äpfel	***ep**-fèl*
	or gate	*ay*	Käse	***kay**-zè*
au	cow	*ow*	braun	*brown*
äu	boy	*oy*	Geräusch	*gè-**roysh***
e	met	*e*	Hotel	*hō-**tel***
	or gate	*ay*	geben	***gay**-bèn*
	or garden	*è*	Woche	***vokh**-è*
ei	wine	i . . . e	Wein	*vine*
	goodbye	or *ye*	frei	*frye*
eu	boy	*oy*	heute	***hoy**-tè*
i	bit	*i*	bitte	***bi**-tè*
	or meet	*ee*	ihn	*een*
ie	meet	*ee*	Sie	*zee*
o	note	*ō*	wo	*vō*
	or not	*o*	Woche	***vokh**-è*
ö	hurt	*ur'*	möchte	***mur'kh**-tè*
u	hook	*oo*	Nuß	*nooss*
ü	see above	*o͞o*	über	***oo**-bèr*
ch	loch (Scottish)	*kh*	Woche	***vokh**-è*
d	date	*d*	die	*dee*
	or cat	*t*	Bad	*baht*
j	yes	*y*	jemand	***yay**-mant*
qu	k + v	*kv*	Qualität	*kva-lee-**tayt***
s	sat	*s* or *ss*	das	*dass*
	or zero	*z*	Sie	*zee*
sch	sh	*sh*	Schuhe	***shoo**-è*
sp	sh + p	*shp*	sprechen	***shprekh**-èn*
ß	loss	*s* or *ss*	Nuß	*nooss*
st	sh + t	*sht*	Stadt	*shtat*
	or last	*st*	nächste	***naykh**-stè*
v	fat	*f*	von	*fon*
w	vine	*v*	Wein	*vine*
z	cats	*ts*	zu	*tsoo*

The syllable to be stressed is the one in **heavy type**.

Everyday Phrases

To start off, a few phrases you can use for basic contact with the German in the street.

Hello – Guten Tag
__goo__-tèn tahk

Good evening – Guten Abend
__goo__-tèn __ah__-bènt

Good night – Gute Nacht
__goo__-tè nakht

Goodbye – Auf Wiedersehen
owf __vee__-dèr-zay-èn

Yes – Ja
yah

No – Nein
nine

O.K. – In Ordnung
in __ord__-noong

How are you? – Wie geht es Ihnen?
vee gayt es __een__-èn?

I'm very well – Es geht mir sehr gut
es gayt meer zer goot

Please – Bitte
__bit__-è

Yes please – Ja, bitte
yah, __bit__-è

Thank you – Danke
__dang__-kè

No thank you – Nein, danke
nine, __dang__-kè

That's very kind of you – Das ist sehr freundlich von Ihnen
dass ist zer __froynt__-likh fon __een__-èn

You're welcome – Keine Ursache!
__kine__-è __oor__-zakh-è!

Everyday Phrases

I'm sorry – Es tut mir leid
es toot meer lite

Excuse me – Entschuldigung
*ent-**shool**-di-goong*

It doesn't matter – Es macht nichts
es makht nikhts

I don't mind – Es ist mir egal
*es ist meer ay-**gahl***

What is your name? – Wie heißen Sie?
*vee **hye**-sèn zee?*

My name is Mark Roberts – Ich heiße Mark Roberts
*ikh **hye**-sè Mark Roberts*

I come from America – Ich komme aus Amerika
*ikh **ko**-mè ows a-**may**-ri-ka*

I come from Britain – Ich komme aus Großbritannien
*ikh **ko**-mè ows grōss-bri-**tan**-i-yen*

I live in Chester – Ich wohne in Chester
*ikh **vō**-nè in Chester*

I am on holiday – Ich bin auf Urlaub
*ikh bin owf **oor**-lowp*

See you soon – Bis bald
bis balt

Your First Questions

You won't go very far before you want to ask questions like these. We may not have given the exact question you need, and you may have to change a few words, but you should manage. The key part of some very common questions is in capitals; you can vary the ending yourself as circumstances require.

I WANT a single room	– ICH HÄTTE GERNE ein Einzelzimmer *ikh **he**-tè **gern**-è ine **ine**-tsèl-tsim-èr*
WE WANT TO buy some souvenirs	– WIR MÖCHTEN ein paar Andenken kaufen *veer **mur'kh**-tèn ine par **an**-deng-kèn **kow**-fèn*
How much does that cost?	– Wieviel kostet das? ***vee**-feel **kos**-tèt dass?*
I WANT TO make a phone call	– ICH MÖCHTE telefonieren *ikh **mur'kh**-tè tay-lay-fo-**nee**-rèn*
I NEED a doctor	– ICH BRAUCHE einen Arzt *ikh **brow**-khè **ine**-èn artst*
WHERE IS the Tourist Information Office?	– WO IST das Fremdenverkehrsamt? *vō ist dass **frem**-dèn-fer-kerz-amt?*
WE ARE LOOKING FOR a camping site	– WIR SUCHEN einen Campingplatz *veer **zoo**-khèn **ine**-èn **kam**-ping-plats*
DO YOU KNOW a good restaurant?	– KENNEN SIE ein gutes Restaurant? ***ken**-èn zee ine **goo**-tès res-tō-**rang**?*
SHOULD WE reserve a table?	– SOLLEN WIR einen Tisch reservieren? ***zol**-èn veer **ine**-èn tish rez-èr-**veer**-èn?*
CAN I rent a car?	– KANN ICH ein Auto mieten? *kan ikh ine **ow**-tō **mee**-tèn?*
How long will it take to repair the car?	– Wie lange wird die Reparatur dauern? *vee **lang**-è veert dee re-pa-ra-**toor** **dow**-ern?*
What time is it please?	– Wieviel Uhr ist es bitte? ***vee**-feel **oo**-èr ist es **bit**-è?*

Your First Questions

WHAT TIME do you close? – UM WIEVIEL UHR schließen Sie?
*oom **vee**-feel **oo**-èr **shlee**-sèn zee?*

WHEN IS THE NEXT TRAIN to Munich? – WANN FÄHRT DER NÄCHSTE ZUG nach München?
*van fert der **naykh**-ste tsook nahkh **mōōn**-khèn?*

MAY I BORROW your pen? – KANN ICH MIR Ihren Kuli AUSLEIHEN?
*kan ikh meer **ee**-rèn **koo**-lee **ows**-lye-èn?*

DO I HAVE TIME to buy a magazine? – HABE ICH NOCH ZEIT, eine Zeitschrift zu kaufen?
***hah**-bè ikh nokh tsite **ine**-è **tsite**-shrift tsoo **kow**-fèn?*

What is this? – Was ist das?
vass ist dass?

Who did this? – Wer hat das gemacht?
*ver hat dass gè-**makht**?*

Who should I see about this? – An wen soll ich mich damit wenden?
*an vayn zol ikh mikh da-**mit** **ven**-dèn?*

HAVE YOU GOT any matches? – HABEN SIE Streichhölzer?
***hah**-bèn zee **shtrye**-khur'l-tsèr?*

Do you mind if I . . . ? – Hätten Sie etwas dagegen, wenn ich . . . ?
***he**-tèn zee **et**-vas da-**gay**-gèn ven ikh . . . ?*

Problems

Of course we hope you won't have any, and that if you do they're minor ones and not real emergencies. The phrases we've given here cover both and are meant to help you through any difficulties that may come along.

Can you help me please? – Können Sie mir bitte helfen?
***kur'n**-èn zee meer **bit**-è **hel**-fèn?*

Would you come with me please? – Würden Sie bitte mit mir kommen?
***vōōr**-dèn zee **bit**-è mit meer **ko**-mèn?*

What is the matter? – Was ist los?
vass ist lōs?

What do you think is wrong? – Was, glauben Sie, stimmt hier nicht?
***vass glow**-bèn zee shtimt heer nikht?*

I don't understand – Ich verstehe nicht
*ikh fer-**shtay**-è nikht*

I don't speak German – Ich spreche kein Deutsch
*ikh **shpre**-khè kine doytsh*

Please repeat that – Wiederholen Sie das, bitte
*vee-dèr-**hō**-lèn zee dass **bit**-è*

I need someone who speaks English – Ich brauche jemanden, der Englisch spricht
*ikh **brow**-khè **yay**-man-dèn der **eng**-lish shprikht*

I haven't enough money – Ich habe nicht genug Geld
*ikh **hah**-bè nikht gè-**nook** gelt*

I have no money – Ich habe kein Geld
*ikh **hah**-bè kine gelt*

Is there somewhere open where we can eat? – Hat hier etwas offen, wo wir essen können?
*hat heer **et**-vas **o**-fèn, vō veer **ess**-èn **kur'n**-èn?*

That man keeps following me – Der Mann geht mir dauernd nach
*der man gayt meer **dow**-ernt nahkh*

Stop following me – Laufen Sie mir nicht dauernd nach!
***low**-fèn zee meer nikht **dow**-ernt nahkh!*

Problems

Call the police – Rufen Sie die Polizei
__roo__-fèn zee dee po-lit-__sye__

My car has been broken into – Jemand hat mein Auto aufgebrochen
__yay__-mant hat mine __ow__-tō __owf__-gè-bro-khèn

My son is lost – Mein Sohn ist verlorengegangen
mine zōn ist fer-__lor__-èn gè-__gang__-èn

Where is the police station? – Wo ist das Polizeirevier?
vō ist dass po-lit-__sye__-re-veer?

I have lost my passport – Ich habe meinen Reisepaß verloren
ikh __hah__-bè __mine__-èn __rye__-zè-pass fer-__lor__-èn

My wallet has been stolen – Meine Brieftasche ist gestohlen worden
__mine__-è __breef__-tash-è ist gè-__shtō__-lèn __vor__-dèn

The insurance company requires me to report it – Ich muß das wegen meiner Versicherung zur Anzeige bringen
ikh moss dass __vay__-gèn __mine__-èr fer-__zikh__-è-roong tsoor __an__-tsye-gè __bring__-èn

I want to see a lawyer – Ich möchte mit einem Anwalt sprechen
ikh __mur'kh__-tè mit __ine__-èm __an__-valt __shpre__-khèn

Please give me my passport back – Bitte geben Sie mir meinen Paß wieder
__bit__-è __gay__-bèn zee meer __mine__-èn pass __vee__-dèr

Where is the British consulate? – Wo ist das britische Konsulat?
vō ist dass __bri__-tish-è kon-zoo-__laht__?

There is a fire – Es brennt
es brent

There has been an accident – Es hat einen Unfall gegeben
es hat __ine__-èn __oon__-fal gè-__gay__-bèn

Call an ambulance – Rufen Sie einen Krankenwagen
__roo__-fèn zee __ine__-èn __krang__-kèn-vah-gèn

Problems

I need a doctor –	Ich brauche einen Arzt *ikh **brow**-khè **ine**-èn artst*
I feel ill –	Ich fühle mich krank *ikh **foo**-lè mikh krank*
He has hurt himself –	Er hat sich verletzt *er hat zikh fer-**letst***
My car won't start –	Mein Auto springt nicht an *mine **ow**-tō shpringt nikht an*
There is something wrong with the brakes –	Mit den Bremsen ist etwas nicht in Ordnung *mit dayn **brem**-zèn ist **et**-vas nikht in **ord**-noong*
The machine is broken –	Die Maschine ist kaputt *dee ma-**shee**-nè ist ka-**poot***
The air-conditioning does not work –	Die Klimaanlage geht nicht *dee **klee**-ma-an-lah-gè gayt nikht*
I am in a hurry –	Ich habe es eilig *ikh **hah**-bè es **ile**-ikh*
I am late –	Ich bin spät dran *ikh bin shpayt drahn*
How long will this take? –	Wie lange wird das dauern? *vee **lang**-è veert dass **dow**-ern?*
How long will the delay be? –	Wie lange wird die Verspätung sein? *vee **lang**-è veert dee fer-**shpay**-toong zine?*
I am leaving tomorrow. Can you do it at once? –	Ich fahre morgen ab. Können Sie es sofort machen? *ikh **fah**-rè **mor**-gèn ap. **kur'n**-èn zee es zō-**fort** **makh**-èn?*
I have forgotten my key –	Ich habe meinen Schlüssel vergessen *ikh **hah**-bè **mine**-èn **shloo**-sèl fer-**ges**-èn*
I have left my bag in the toilet (restroom) –	Ich habe meine Tasche in der Toilette gelassen *ikh **hah**-bè **mine**-è **tash**-è in der tō-a-**le**-tè gè-**las**-èn*

Problems

My luggage has not arrived –	Mein Gepäck ist noch nicht angekommen *mine gè-**pek** ist nokh nikht **an**-gè-ko-mèn*
I have missed my train –	Ich habe meinen Zug verpaßt *ikh **hah**-bè **mine**-èn tsook fer-**past***
The people who were to meet me have not turned up –	Die Leute, die mich abholen sollten, sind nicht gekommen *dee **loy**-tè dee mikh **ap**-hō-lèn **zol**-tèn zint nikht gè-**ko**-mèn*
My party has left without me –	Meine Gruppe ist ohne mich weggegangen ***mine**-è **groo**-pè ist **ō**-nè mikh **vek**-gè-gang-èn*
I have lost my way. How do I get to the station? –	Ich habe mich verlaufen. Wie komme ich bitte zum Bahnhof? *ikh **hah**-bè mikh fer-**low**-fèn. vee **ko**-mè ikh **bit**-è tsoom **bahn**-hōf?*
I have broken my glasses –	Ich habe meine Brille kaputt gemacht *ikh **hah**-bè **mine**-è **bri**-lè ka-**poot** gè-**mahkht***
I have spilt something –	Ich habe etwas verschüttet *ikh **hah**-bè **et**-vas fer-**shōō**-tèt*
My clothes are soaked Where can I dry them? –	Meine Kleider sind völlig durchnäßt. Wo kann ich sie trocknen? ***mine**-è **klye**-dèr zint **fur'**-likh doorkh-**nest**. vō kan ikh zee **trok**-nèn?*

When You Arrive
The Formalities

Entering Germany is usually a simple business. You may possibly be stopped and asked a few questions – the answers given here should be adequate.

Here is my passport – Hier ist mein Paß
heer ist mine pass

My wife and I are on a joint passport – Meine Frau und ich haben einen gemeinsamen Paß
***mine**-è frow oont ikh **hah**-bèn **ine**-èn gè-**mine**-zahm-èn pass*

Here is my driving licence and green card – Hier sind mein Führerschein und meine grüne Versicherungskarte
*heer zint mine **foo**-rèr-shine oont **mine**-è **grōō**-nè fer-**zikh**-è-roongz-kar-tè*

I am staying for two weeks – Ich bleibe zwei Wochen
*ikh **blye**-bè tsvye **vo**-khèn*

We are visiting some friends – Wir besuchen ein paar Freunde
*veer bè-**zoo**-khèn ine par **froyn**-dè*

I have nothing to declare – Ich habe nichts zu verzollen
*ikh **hah**-bè nikhts tsoo fer-**tsol**-èn*

I have the usual allowances of tobacco and spirits (liquor) – Ich habe die übliche Menge an zollfreien Tabakwaren und Alkohol
*ikh **hah**-bè dee **ōō**-blikh-è **meng**-è an **tsol**-frye-èn ta-**bak**-vah-rèn oont **al**-ko-hol*

That is for my personal use – Das ist für meinen persönlichen Bedarf
*dass ist fōōr **mine**-èn per-**zur'n**-likh-èn bè-**darf***

How much do I have to pay? – Wieviel muß ich dafür zahlen?
***vee**-feel mooss ikh da-**fōōr tsah**-lèn?*

Is there a bus into town? – Gibt es einen Bus in die Stadt?
*gipt es **ine**-èn booss in dee shtat?*

Where do I get the connecting flight to Cologne? – Von wo aus nehme ich die Anschlußmaschine nach Köln?
*fon vō ows **nay**-mè ikh dee **an**-shlooss-ma-shee-nè nahkh kur'ln?*

When You Arrive
Your Luggage

Where is the luggage from the London flight? – Wo ist das Gepäck vom Flug aus London?
*vō ist dass gè-**pek** fom flook ows **lon**-don?*

My suitcase is stuck on the conveyor belt – Mein Koffer ist auf dem Förderband steckengeblieben
*mine **ko**-fèr ist owf daym **fur'**-dèr-bant **shte**-kèn-gè-**blee**-bèn*

Are there any porters? – Gibt es hier Gepäckträger?
*gipt es heer gè-**pek**-tray-gèr?*

Are there any luggage trolleys? – Gibt es hier Kofferkulis?
*gipt es heer **ko**-fèr-koo-leez?*

Is there any charge? – Kostet das etwas?
***kos**-tèt dass **et**-vas?*

Is there a left-luggage office (baggage room)? – Gibt es hier eine Gepäckaufbewahrung?
*gipt es heer **ine**-è gè-**pek**-owf-bè-**vah**-roong?*

Please take these bags to a taxi – Bitte bringen Sie diese Taschen zu einem Taxi
***bit**-è **bring**-èn zee **dee**-zè **tash**-èn tsoo **ine**-èm **tak**-see*

I'll carry that myself – Das trage ich selbst
*dass **trah**-gè ikh zelpst*

Careful, the handle is broken – Vorsicht bitte, der Griff ist kaputt
for**-zikht **bit**-è, der grif ist ka-**poot

No, don't put that on top! – Nein, legen Sie das bitte nicht obendrauf!
*nine, **lay**-gèn zee dass **bit**-è nikht **ō**-bèn-drowf!*

These bags are not mine – Diese Taschen gehören mir nicht
***dee**-zè **tash**-èn gè-**hur'**-èn meer nikht*

Where is my other suitcase? – Wo ist mein anderer Koffer?
*vō ist mine **an**-dè-rèr **ko**-fèr?*

Asking the Way
Things you'll hear

It's no use being able to ask the way if you're not going to understand the directions you get. We've tried to anticipate the likely answers, so listen carefully for these key phrases.

Gehen Sie immer geradeaus weiter – Keep going straight ahead
***gay**-èn zee **i**-mèr gè-**rah**-dè-ows **vye**-tèr*

Kehren Sie um – You have to turn around
***ker**-rèn zee oom*

Gehen Sie – **in Richtung . . .**
***gay**-èn zee* – *in **rikh**-toong . . .*
You go – towards . . .

– **nach rechts**
nahkh rekhts
right

– **nach links**
nahkh links
left

– **bis zu . . .**
biss tsoo . . .
as far as . . .

Biegen Sie – **rechts ab**
***bee**-gèn zee* – *rekhts ap*
Turn – right

– **links ab**
links ap
left

Nehmen Sie – **die erste (Straße) rechts**
***nay**-mèn zee* – *dee **ers**-tè (**shtrah**-sè) rekhts*
Take – the first (road) on the right

– **die zweite (Straße) links**
*dee **tsvye**-tè (**shtrah**-sè) links*
the second (road) on the left

– **die Straße nach . . .**
*dee **shtrah**-sè nahkh . . .*
the road for . . .

Asking the Way
Things you'll hear

Folgen Sie den Schildern nach . . . – Follow the signs for . . .
*fol-gèn zee dayn **shil**-dèrn nahkh . . .*

Gehen Sie über – **die Straße**
*gay-èn zee **oo**-ber* – *dee **shtrah**-sè*
Cross – the street

– **den Platz**
dayn plats
the square

– **den Bahnübergang**
*dayn **bahn**-oo-ber-gang*
the level (grade) crossing

Es ist – **an der Kreuzung**
es ist – *an der **kroy**-tsoong*
It's – at the junction (intersection)

– **nach der Ampel**
*nahkh der **am**-pèl*
after the traffic lights

– **da drüben**
*da **droo**-bèn*
over there

– **um die Ecke**
*oom dee **e**-kè*
around the corner

– **gegenüber der Kirche**
***gay**-gèn-oo-ber der **keer**-khè*
opposite the church

– **beim Theater**
*bime tay-**ah**-tèr*
next to the theatre

– **im nächsten Stock**
*im **naykh**-stèn shtok*
on the next floor

Asking the Way

Excuse me, please –	Entschuldigen Sie, bitte *ent-**shool**-di-gèn zee, **bit**-è*
Where is the cathedral? –	Wo ist der Dom? *vō ist der dōm?*
Can you tell me the way to the airport? –	Können Sie mir sagen, wie ich zum Flughafen komme? ***kur'n**-èn zee meer **zah**-gèn vee ikh tsoom **flook**-hah-fèn **ko**-mè?*
Where are the toilets? –	Wo sind die Toiletten? *vō zint dee tō-a-**le**-tèn?*
Is there a service station near here? –	Gibt es hier in der Nähe eine Tankstelle? *gipt es heer in der **nay**-è **ine**-è **tank**-shte-lè?*
Where is the nearest post office? –	Wo ist das nächste Postamt? *vō ist dass **naykhs**-tè **post**-amt?*
Is this the right way to the castle? –	Ist das der richtige Weg zum Schloß? *ist dass der **rikh**-ti-gè vayg tsoom shloss?*
How long will it take to get there? –	Wie lange braucht man dahin? *vee **lang**-è browkht man dah-**hin**?*
Is it far? –	Ist es weit? *ist es vite?*
Can you walk there? –	Kann man zu Fuß hingehen? *kan man tsoo fooss **hin**-gay-èn?*
Is there a bus that goes there? –	Fährt ein Bus dahin? *fert ine booss dah-**hin**?*
Is there a train that goes there? –	Gibt es einen Zug dahin? *gipt es **ine**-èn tsook dah-**hin**?*
Where do I get the bus for Frankfurt? –	Wo fährt der Bus nach Frankfurt ab? *vō fert der booss nahkh **frank**-foort ap?*
I am trying to get to the centre of the city –	Ich versuche, ins Stadtzentrum zu kommen *ikh fer-**zoo**-khè ins **shtat**-tsen-troom tsoo **ko**-mèn*

Asking the Way

I have lost my way –	Ich habe mich verlaufen *ikh **hah**-bè mikh fer-**low**-fèn*
I am looking for the Tourist Information Office –	Ich suche das Fremdenverkehrsamt *ikh **zoo**-khè dass **frem**-dèn-fer-kerz-amt*
Can you show me on the map? –	Können Sie mir das auf der Karte zeigen? ***kur'n**-èn zee meer dass owf der **kar**-tè **tsye**-gèn?*
Which road do I take for Cologne? –	Welche Straße muß ich nach Köln nehmen? ***vel**-khè **shtrah**-sè mooss ikh nahkh kur'ln **nay**-mèn?*
How far is it to Hamburg? –	Wie weit ist es nach Hamburg? *vee vite ist es nahkh **ham**-boork?*
Will we arrive by this evening? –	Sind wir bis heute abend dort? *sind veer biss **hoy**-tè **ah**-bènt dort?*
Which is the best route to Stuttgart? –	Welches ist die beste Strecke nach Stuttgart? ***vel**-khèss ist dee **bes**-tè **shtre**-kè nahkh **shtoot**-gart?*
Which is the most scenic route? –	Welches ist die landschaftlich schönste Strecke? ***vel**-khèss ist dee **lant**-shaft-likh **shur'n**-stè **shtre**-kè?*
Do I turn here for Hamburg? –	Muß ich hier nach Hamburg abbiegen? *mooss ikh heer nahkh **ham**-boork **ap**-bee-gèn?*
Is the traffic one-way? –	Ist es eine Einbahnstraße? *ist es **ine**-è **ine**-bahn-shtrah-sè?*
How do I get onto the motorway (highway)? –	Wie komme ich auf die Autobahn? *vee **ko**-mè ikh owf dee **ow**-tō-bahn?*
Where does this road go to? –	Wo führt diese Straße hin? *vō foort **dee**-zè **shtrah**-sè hin?*

Buses

Most cities have a pay-as-you-enter bus system, with a standard fare for all journeys. You can make a saving by buying your tickets in packs of ten – ask for *ein Fahrscheinheft* – or a 7-day tourist ticket. You cancel your own ticket in a machine as you go in. There are underground railways in several cities like Berlin, Frankfurt and Munich, and the same tickets can be used.

Which bus do I take for the museum? – Mit welchem Bus komme ich zum Museum?
mit ***vel****-khèm booss* ***ko****-mè ikh tsoom moo-****zay****-oom?*

Where do I get the bus for the airport? – Wo fährt der Bus zum Flughafen ab?
vō fert der booss tsoom ***flook****-hah-fèn ap?*

Does this bus go to the Deutsche Theater? – Fährt dieser Bus zum Deutschen Theater?
fert ***dee****-zèr booss tsoom* ***doyt****-shèn tay-****ah****-tèr?*

Where should I change? – Wo muß ich umsteigen?
vō mooss ikh ***oom****-shtye-gèn?*

I want to go to the cathedral – Ich möchte zum Dom
ikh ***mur'kh****-tè tsoom dōm*

A 7-day tourist ticket, please – Eine Touristen-Wochenkarte, bitte!
ine*-è too-****ris****-tèn-****vo****-khèn-kar-tè,* ***bit****-è*

Will you let me off at the right stop? – Sagen Sie mir, wann ich aussteigen muß?
zah*-gèn zee meer van ikh* ***ows****-shtye-gèn mooss?*

What is the fare to the centre of the city? – Was kostet die Fahrt ins Stadtzentrum?
vass ***kos****-tèt-dee fart ins* ***shtat****-tsen-troom?*

When is the last bus? – Wann geht der letzte Bus?
van gayt der ***let****-stè booss?*

How long does it take to get to the museum? – Wie lange fährt man zum Museum?
vee ***lang****-è fert man tsoom moo-****zay****-oom?*

How frequent is the service? – Wie oft fährt hier etwas?
vee oft fert heer ***et****-vas?*

Taxis

Taxis can be picked up at a stand or hailed. They may not stop if they are too close to a stand. A tip of about one D.Mark is expected.

The main station, please – Zum Hauptbahnhof, bitte
*tsoom **howpt**-bahn-hōf, **bit**-è*

30, Gartenstraße, please – Zur Gartenstraße dreißig, bitte
*tsoor **gar**-tèn-shtrah-sè **drye**-sikh, **bit**-è*

Please take me to this address – Bitte fahren Sie mich zu dieser Adresse
***bit**-è **fah**-rèn zee mikh tsoo **dee**-zèr a-**dress**-è*

Take me to the airport, please – Zum Flughafen, bitte
*tsoom **flook**-hah-fèn **bit**-è*

Will you put the luggage in the boot (trunk)? – Könnten Sie das Gepäck in den Kofferraum legen?
***kur'n**-tèn zee dass gè-**pek** in dayn **ko**-fèr-rowm **lay**-gèn?*

Please drive us around the town – Bitte fahren Sie uns in der Stadt herum
bit**-è **fah**-rèn zee oons in der shtat hèr-**oom

I'm in a hurry – Ich habe es eilig
*ikh **hah**-bè es **ile**-ikh*

Please wait here for a few minutes – Bitte warten Sie hier ein paar Minuten
***bit**-è **var**-tèn zee heer ine par mi-**noo**-tèn*

Turn left, please – Biegen Sie bitte links ab
***bee**-gèn zee **bit**-è links ap*

Turn right, please – Biegen Sie bitte rechts ab
***bee**-gèn zee **bit**-è rekhts ap*

Please stop at the corner – Bitte halten Sie an der Ecke
***bit**-è **hal**-tèn zee an der **e**-kè*

How much is that, please? – Wieviel macht das bitte?
***vee**-feel makht dass **bit**-è?*

Keep the change – Der Rest ist für Sie
der rest ist fōōr zee

Trains
Your Ticket

The railways provide an excellent way of seeing the country. On the de luxe Inter-City trains you will have to pay an extra charge on top of the normal fare. Children under ten pay half fare, and those under four travel free.

If you are taking an overnight train you can reserve either a sleeper or a couchette, which is a simple berth with blankets in a compartment shared by several passengers.

A single (one-way ticket) to Frankfurt, please – Einmal einfach nach Frankfurt, bitte
__ine__-mal __ine__-fakh nahkh __frank__-foort, __bit__-è

A return (round-trip ticket) to Frankfurt, please – Eine Rückfahrkarte nach Frankfurt, bitte
__ine__-è __rōōk__-far-kar-tè nahkh __frank__-foort, __bit__-è

A child's return to Frankfurt, please – Eine Kinderrückfahrkarte nach Frankfurt, bitte
__ine__-è __kin__-dèr-rōōk-far-kar-tè nahkh __frank__-foort, __bit__-è

A return to Frankfurt, first class – Eine Rückfahrkarte erster Klasse nach Frankfurt, bitte
__ine__-è __rōōk__-far-kar-tè __ers__-tèr __kla__-sè nahkh __frank__-foort, __bit__-è

I want to book a seat on the 10.30 to Hamburg – Ich möchte eine Platzkarte für den Zug um zehn Uhr dreißig nach Hamburg
ikh __mur'kh__-tè __ine__-è __plats__-kar-tè fōōr dayn tsook oom tsayn __oo__-èr __drye__-sikh nahkh __ham__-boork

Second class, by the window – Zweite Klasse, Fensterplatz
__tsvye__-tè __kla__-sè, __fen__-stèr-plats

A smoking compartment, first class – Ein Raucherabteil, erste Klasse
ine __row__-khèr-ap-tile, __ers__-tè __kla__-sè

A no-smoking compartment, please – Ein Nichtraucherabteil, bitte
ine __nikht__-row-khèr-ap-tile __bit__-è

Trains
Your Luggage

Can I have a sleeper on the 2200 to Hamburg?	– Kann ich einen Schlafwagenplatz für den Zug um zweiundzwanzig Uhr nach Hamburg haben? *kan ikh **ine**-èn **shlahf**-vah-gèn-plats fōōr dayn tsook oom **tsvye**-oont-tsvan-tsikh **oo**-èr nahkh **ham**-boork **hah**-bèn?*
Can I have a couchette on the 2200 to Hamburg?	– Kann ich einen Liegewagenplatz für den Zug um zweiundzwanzig Uhr nach Hamburg haben? *kan ikh **ine**-èn **lee**-gè-vah-gèn-plats fōōr dayn tsook oom **tsvye**-oont-tsvan-tsikh **oo**-èr nahkh **ham**-boork **hah**-bèn?*
Can I register (check) my luggage?	– Kann ich mein Gepäck aufgeben? *kan ikh mine gè-**pek owf**-gay-bèn?*
I want to register (check) these bags	– Ich möchte diese Taschen aufgeben *ikh **mur'kh**-tè **dee**-zè **tash**-èn **owf**-gay-bèn*
Where do I pick up my registered (checked) luggage?	– Wo kann ich mein Gepäck abholen? *vō kan ikh mine gè-**pek ap**-hō-lèn?*
I want to leave these bags in the left luggage (baggage room)	– Ich möchte diese Taschen in der Gepäckaufbewahrung lassen *ikh **mur'kh**-tè **dee**-zè **tash**-èn in der gè-**pek**-owf-bè-vah-roong **la**-sèn*
I shall pick them up this evening	– Ich hole sie heute abend wieder ab *ikh **hō**-lè zee **hoy**-tè **ah**-bènt **vee**-dèr ap*
What time do you close?	– Wann machen Sie zu? *van **makh**-èn zee tsoo?*
How much is it per suitcase?	– Wieviel kostet es pro Koffer? ***vee**-feel **kos**-tèt es prō **ko**-fèr?*
Please take these bags to platform 9	– Bitte bringen Sie diese Taschen zum Bahnsteig neun ***bit**-è **bring**-èn zee **dee**-zè **tash**-èn tsoom **bahn**-shtike noyn*

Trains
Boarding the Train

Would you look after these cases for a minute please?	Würden Sie bitte eine Minute auf diese Koffer aufpassen? ***voor**-dèn zee **bit**-è **ine**-è mi-**noo**-tè owf **dee**-zè **ko**-fèr **owf**-pa-sèn?*
Where is the departure board (listing)?	Wo ist die Abfahrtstafel? *vō ist dee **ap**-farts-tah-fèl?*
When is the next train to Hamburg?	Wann geht der nächste Zug nach Hamburg? *van gayt der **naykh**-stè tsook nahkh **ham**-boork?*
What are the times of trains to Cologne?	Was sind die Abfahrtszeiten der Züge nach Köln? *vass zint dee **ap**-farts-tsye-tèn der **tsoo**-gè nahkh kur'ln?*
What time is the last train to Stuttgart?	Wann geht der letzte Zug nach Stuttgart? *van gayt der **let**-stè tsook nahkh **shtoot**-gart?*
What platform do I go to for the Hamburg train?	Von welchem Bahnsteig fährt der Zug nach Hamburg ab? *fon **vel**-khèn **bahn**-shtike fert der tsook nahkh **ham**-boork ap?*
Is this the platform for Hamburg?	Fährt der Zug nach Hamburg von diesem Bahnsteig ab? *fert der tsook nahkh **ham**-boork fon **dee**-zèm **bahn**-shtike ap?*
Is this the Hamburg train?	Ist das der Zug nach Hamburg? *ist dass der tsook nahkh **ham**-boork?*
What time does the train leave?	Wann fährt der Zug ab? *vann fert der tsook ap?*
Is there a dining car?	Gibt es einen Speisewagen? *gipt es **ine**-èn **shpye**-zè-vah-gèn?*
Is there a buffet car (club car)?	Gibt es einen Büffetwagen? *gipt es **ine**-èn boo-**fay**-vah-gèn?*
What time do we get to Hamburg?	Wann kommen wir in Hamburg an? *vann **ko**-mèn veer in **ham**-boork an?*

Trains
In the Train

Do we stop at Hannover? –	Halten wir in Hannover? ***hal**-tèn veer in ha-**nō**-fèr?*
Is this a through train? –	Ist das ein durchgehender Zug? *ist dass ine doorkh-**gay**-èn-dèr tsook?*
Where do I have to change (for Bremen)? –	Wo muß ich (nach Bremen) umsteigen? *vō mooss ikh (nahkh **bray**-mèn) **oom**-shtye-gèn?*
How long do I have before my next train leaves? –	Wieviel Zeit habe ich noch bis mein Anschlußzug geht? ***vee**-feel tsite **hah**-bè ikh biss mine **an**-shlooss-tsook gayt?*
Is this seat taken? –	Ist dieser Platz besetzt? *ist **dee**-zèr plats bè-**zetst**?*
This is my seat –	Das ist mein Platz *dass ist mine plats*
Can you help me with my bags please? –	Können Sie mir bitte mit meinem Gepäck helfen? ***kur'n**-èn zee meer **bit**-è mit **mine**-èm gè-**pek hel**-fèn?*
May I open the window? –	Darf ich das Fenster aufmachen? *darf ikh dass **fen**-stèr **owf**-makh-èn?*
This is a no-smoking compartment –	Das ist ein Nichtraucherabteil *dass ist ine **nikht**-row-khèr-ap-tile*
My wife has my ticket –	Meine Frau hat meine Fahrkarte ***mine**-è frow hat **mine**-è **far**-kar-tè*
Are we at Bonn yet? –	Sind wir schon in Bonn? *zint veer shōn in bon?*
Are we on time? –	Ist der Zug pünktlich? *ist der tsook **pōōngt**-likh?*

Driving
Service Station

Benzin – petrol or gas – comes in two varieties in Germany: *Normal* (= 3 star) and *Super* (= 4 Star). We've set out conversion tables for you to work out how many litres to ask for, and to tell you what your metric tyre pressure should be.

15 litres of – **3 star**
Fünfzehn Liter Normal
foonf**-tsayn **lee**-tèr* *nor-**mahl

– **4 star**
Super
***zoo**-pèr*

– **diesel fuel**
Diesel
***dee**-zèl*

20 D.Marks worth please – Für zwanzig Mark, bitte
*foor **tsvan**-tsikh mark, **bit**-è*

Fill her up please – Volltanken, bitte
***fol**-tang-kèn, **bit**-è*

Check – **the oil**
Prüfen Sie den Ölstand
***proo**-fèn zee* *dayn **ur'l**-shtant*

– **the water**
das Kühlwasser
*dass **kool**-vass-er*

I need some distilled water – Ich brauche etwas destilliertes Wasser
*ikh **brow**-khè **et**-vas des-til-**eer**-tès **vass**-er*

Check the tyre pressure please – Prüfen Sie bitte den Reifendruck nach
***proo**-fèn zee **bit**-è dayn **rye**-fèn-drook nahkh*

The pressure should be 2.3 – Der Reifendruck soll zwei Komma drei atü betragen
*der **rye**-fèn-drook zol tsvye **ko**-ma drye a-**too** bè-**trah**-gèn*

Driving
Parking

Some German cities have adopted the system of the disc zone. You just leave a parking disc by your windscreen, and this shows when you arrived and when you should leave. Elsewhere you will find parking meters, as well as streets where parking is only allowed on one side on a given day, depending on whether it is an odd- or even-numbered date.

Can I park here? – Kann ich hier parken?
kan ikh heer ***par****-kèn?*

Where is there a car park (parking lot)? – Wo ist hier ein Parkplatz?
vō ist heer ine ***park****-plats?*

Do I need a parking disc? – Brauche ich eine Parkscheibe?
brow*-khè ikh* ***ine****-è* ***park****-shye-bè?*

Where can I get a parking disc? – Wo kann ich eine Parkscheibe bekommen?
vō kan ikh ***ine****-è* ***park****-shye-bè bè-****ko****-mèn?*

Do I need parking lights? – Muß ich das Standlicht anlassen?
mooss ikh dass ***shtant****-likht* ***an****-la-sèn?*

What time does the car park close? – Wann wird der Parkplatz geschlossen?
van veert der ***park****-plats gè-****shlo****-sèn?*

How long can I stay here? – Wie lange kann ich hier parken?
vee ***lang****-è kan ikh heer* ***par****-kèn?*

Tyre Pressures

lb/sq in	15	18	20	22	24	26	28	30	33	35
kg/sq cm	1.1	1.3	1.4	1.5	1.7	1.8	2	2.1	2.3	2.5

Litres	UK Gallons	US Gallons	Litres	UK Gallons	US Gallons
5	1.1	1.3	25	5.5	6.5
10	2.2	2.6	30	6.6	7.8
15	3.3	3.9	35	7.7	9.1
20	4.4	5.2	40	8.8	10.4

Driving
Road Conditions

German roads are usually very good. The only serious problems you're likely to meet are peak traffic in summer months, or heavy snow if you're off on a winter sports trip. The German traffic authorities signpost alternative routes on minor roads with blue signs, and in winter tyre chains may be compulsory.

WARNING! Traffic from the right always has right of way unless you see the *Vorfahrtsstraße* sign shown inside the back cover of this book.

Is the traffic heavy? – Ist der Verkehr stark?
*ist der fer-**ker** shtark?*

Are there any hold-ups (tie-ups)? – Gibt es Staus?
gipt es shtowz?

What's causing this hold-up? – Warum gibt es einen Stau?
***vah**-room gipt es **ine**-èn shtow?*

When will the road be clear? – Wann wird die Straße wieder frei sein?
*van veert dee **shtrah**-sè **vee**-dèr frye zine?*

Is there a detour? – Gibt es eine Umleitung?
*gipt es **ine**-è **oom**-lye-toong?*

What is the speed limit? – Was ist die Höchstgeschwindigkeit?
*vass ist dee **hur'khst**-gè-shvin-dikh-kite?*

Is there a toll on this motorway (highway)? – Ist diese Autobahn gebührenpflichtig?
*ist **dee**-zè **ow**-tō-bahn gè-**bōō**-ren-pflikh-tikh?*

Is the road to Garmisch snowed up? – Ist die Straße nach Garmisch zugeschneit?
*ist dee **shtrah**-sè nahkh **gar**-mish **tsoo**-gè-shnite?*

Is the pass open? – Ist der Paß offen?
*ist der pass **o**-fèn?*

Do I need chains? – Brauche ich Schneeketten?
***brow**-khè ikh **shnay**-ke-tèn?*

Driving
Renting a Car

I want to rent a car – Ich möchte ein Auto mieten
*ikh **mur'kh**-tè ine **ow**-tō **mee**-tèn*

I want it for 5 days – Ich brauche es für fünf Tage
*ikh **brow**-khè es foor foonf **tah**-gè*

Is there a charge for mileage? – Berechnen Sie Kilometergeld?
*bè-**rekh**-nèn zee kee-lō-**may**-tèr-gelt?*

Do you have – **a larger car?**
Haben Sie – ein größeres Auto?
***hah**-bèn zee* – *ine **grur'**-sèr-ès **ow**-tō?*

– **a cheaper car?**
ein billigeres Auto?
*ine **bil**-ig-èr-es **ow**-tō?*

– **an automatic?**
eines mit Automatik?
***ine**-ès mit ow-tō-**mah**-tik?*

My wife will be driving as well – Meine Frau wird auch fahren
***mine**-è frow veert owkh **fah**-rèn*

Must I return the car here? – Muß ich das Auto wieder hierher zurückbringen?
*mooss ikh dass **ow**-tō **vee**-dèr heer-**her** tsoo-**rōōk** **bring**-èn?*

I would like to leave the car in Munich – Ich würde das Auto gerne in München zurückgeben
*ikh **vōōr**-dè dass **ow**-tō **gern**-è in **mōōn**-khèn tsoo-**rōōk**-gay-bèn*

Please show me how to – **operate the lights**
Bitte zeigen Sie mir – wie ich das Licht einschalte
***bit**-è **tsye**-gèn zee meer* – *vee ikh dass likht **ine**-shal-tè*

– **operate the windscreen wipers**
wie ich die Scheibenwischer einschalte
*vee ikh dee **shye**-bèn-vi-shèr **ine**-shal-tè*

Where is the reverse? – Wo ist der Rückwärtsgang?
*vō ist der **rōōk**-verts-gang?*

Please explain the car documents – Bitte erklären Sie mir die Wagenpapiere
***bit**-è er-**klayr**-èn zee meer dee **vah**-gèn-pa-peer-è*

Driving
Breakdowns & Repairs

You should take a red warning triangle and a warning light with you in case of any breakdowns or accidents.

I have had a breakdown – Ich habe eine Panne
ikh ***hah****-bè* ***ine****-è* ***pa****-nè*

Can you send – **a mechanic?**
Können Sie einen Mechaniker schicken?
kur'n*-èn zee* ***ine****-èn mekh-****ah****-ni-kèr* ***shi****-kèn?*

– **a breakdown van (a tow-truck)?**
einen Abschleppwagen schicken?
ine*-èn* ***ap****-shlep-vah-gèn* ***shi****-kèn?*

Can you take me to the nearest garage? – Können Sie mich zur nächsten Werkstatt bringen?
kur'n*-èn zee mikh zoor* ***naykh****-stèn* ***verk****-shtat* ***bring****-èn?*

Can you give me a tow? – Können Sie mich abschleppen?
kur'n*-èn zee mikh* ***ap****-shlep-èn?*

I have run out of petrol (gas) – Ich habe kein Benzin mehr
ikh ***hah****-bè kine ben-****tseen*** *mer*

Can you give me a can of petrol please? – Können Sie mir bitte einen Kanister Benzin geben?
kur'n*-èn zee meer* ***bit****-è* ***ine****-èn ka-****nis****-tèr ben-****tseen gay****-bèn?*

I have lost the ignition key – Ich habe den Zündschlüssel verloren
ikh ***hah****-bè dayn* ***tsōōnt****-shlōō-sèl fer-****lor****-èn*

There is something wrong with my car – Mit meinem Auto ist etwas nicht in Ordnung
mit ***mine****-èm* ***ow****-tō ist* ***et****-vas nikht in* ***ord****-noong*

Can you find the trouble? – Können Sie mal nachsehen?
kur'n*-èn zee mal* ***nahkh****-zay-èn?*

I have a flat tyre – Ich habe einen Platten
ikh ***hah****-bè* ***ine****-èn* ***pla****-tèn*

The battery is dead – Die Batterie ist leer
*dee ba-tè-****ree*** *ist* ***lay****-èr*

Motoring
Breakdowns & Repairs

My windscreen (windshield) has shattered – Meine Windschutzscheibe ist gesprungen
__mine__-è __vint__-shoots-shye-bè ist gè-__shproong__-èn

The engine's overheating – Der Motor wird zu heiß
der __mō__-tor veert tsoo hice

There is a leak in the radiator – Der Kühler ist leck
der __ko͞o__-lèr ist lek

I have blown a fuse – Die Sicherung ist durchgebrannt
dee __zi__-khè-roong ist __doorkh__-gè-brant

The exhaust pipe has fallen off – Der Auspuff ist abgebrochen
der __ows__-poof ist __ap__-gè-bro-khèn

There is a bad connection – Da ist ein Wackelkontakt
dah ist ine __va__-kèl-kon-takt

I need a new fan belt – Ich brauche einen Keilriemen
ikh __brow__-khè __ine__-èn __kile__-ree-mèn

Can you replace the windscreen wiper? – Können Sie den Scheibenwischer auswechseln?
__kur'n__-èn zee dayn __shye__-bèn-vish-èr __ows__-vekh-sèln?

Is it serious? – Ist es etwas Ernstes?
ist es __et__-vas __ern__-stès?

How long will it take to repair it? – Wie lange wird die Reparatur dauern?
vee __lang__-è veert dee re-pa-ra-__toor__ __dow__-ern?

Do you have the parts? – Haben Sie Ersatzteile?
__hah__-bèn zee er-__zats__-tye-lè?

Can you fix it for the time being? – Können Sie es provisorisch reparieren?
__kur'n__-èn zee es pro-vi-__zor__-ish re-pa-__ree__-rèn?

Can I have an itemized bill for my insurance company? – Kann ich eine detaillierte Rechnung für meine Versicherung haben?
kan ikh __ine__-è day-ta-__yeer__-tè __rekh__ noong fo͞or __mine__-è fer-__zi__-khè-roong __hah__-bèn?

Driving The Car

English	German	Pronunciation
accelerator	Gaspedal	***gahs***-*pe-dahl*
air filter	Luftfilter	***looft***-*fil-tèr*
alternator	Stromerzeuger	***shtrōm***-*er-tsoy-gèr*
anti-freeze	Frostschutzmittel	***frost***-*shoots-mi-tèl*
automatic transmission	Automatik	*ow-tō-**mah**-tik*
axle	Achse	***akh***-*sè*
backup light	Rückfahrlicht	***ro͞ok***-*far-likht*
battery	Batterie	*ba-tè-**ree***
bonnet	Motorhaube	***mō***-*tor-how-bè*
boot	Kofferraum	***ko***-*fèr-rowm*
brakes	Bremsen	***brem***-*zèn*
brake fluid	Bremsflüssigkeit	***bremz***-*flo͞o-sikh-kite*
bumper	Stoßstange	***shtōss***-*shtang-è*
carburettor	Vergaser	*fer-**gah**-zèr*
choke	Choke	*chōk*
clutch	Kupplung	***koop***-*loong*
cooling system	Kühlung	***ko͞o***-*loong*
cylinder	Zylinder	*tso͞o-**lin**-dèr*
disc brake	Scheibenbremse	***shye***-*bèn-brem-zè*
distributor	Verteiler	*fer-**tye**-lèr*
door	Tür	*to͞or*
dynamo	Lichtmaschine	***likht***-*ma-shee-nè*
electrical system	elektrische Anlage	*e-**lek**-trish-è **an**-lah-gè*
engine	Motor	***mō***-*tor*
exhaust system	Auspuffanlage	***ows***-*poof-**an**-lah-gè*
fan belt	Keilriemen	***kile***-*ree-mèn*
fuel gauge	Benzinuhr	*ben-**tseen**-oo-èr*
fuel pump	Benzinpumpe	*ben-**tseen**-poom-pè*
fuse	Sicherung	***zikh***-*è-roong*
gear box	Getriebegehäuse	*gè-**tree**-bè-gè-hoy-zè*
gear lever (shift)	Schalthebel	***shalt***-*hay-bèl*
generator	Lichtmaschine	***likht***-*ma-shee-nè*
handbrake	Handbremse	***hant***-*brem-zè*
headlights	Scheinwerfer	***shine***-*ver-fèr*
heating system	Heizung	***hye***-*tsoong*
horn	Hupe	***hoo***-*pè*
hood	Motorhaube	***mō***-*tor-how-bè*
hose	Schlauch	*shlowkh*
ignition	Zündung	***tso͞on***-*doong*
ignition key	Zündschlüssel	***tso͞ont***-*shlo͞o-sèl*

Driving The Car

indicator	Blinker	***bling**-kèr*
jack	Wagenheber	***vah**-gèn-hay-bèr*
lights	Lichtanlage	***likht**-an-lah-gè*
muffler	Auspufftopf	***ows**-poof-topf*
oil	Öl	*ur'l*
oil filter	Ölfilter	***ur'l**-fil-tèr*
oil pressure gauge	Öldruckmesser	***ur'l**-drook-me-sèr*
petrol	Benzin	*ben-**tseen***
radiator	Kühler	***kōō**-lèr*
rear-view mirror	Rückspiegel	***rōōk**-shpee-gèl*
reversing light	Rückfahrlicht	***rōōk**-far-likht*
seat	Sitz	*zits*
seatbelt	Sicherheitsgurt	***zikh**-èr-hites-goort*
shock absorber	Stoßdämpfer	***shtōss**-demp-fèr*
silencer	Auspufftopf	***ows**-poof-topf*
spanner	Schraubenschlüssel	***shrow**-bèn-shlōō-sèl*
spare part	Ersatzteil	*er-**zats**-tile*
spark plug	Zündkerze	***tsōōnt**-ker-tsè*
speedometer	Tachometer	*takh-ō-**may**-tèr*
starter motor	Anlasser	***an**-lass-èr*
steering	Lenkung	***leng**-koong*
stoplight	Bremslicht	***bremz**-likht*
suspension	Aufhängung	***owf**-heng-oong*
transmission	Getriebe	*gè-**tree**-bè*
trunk	Kofferraum	***ko**-fèr-rowm*
turn indicator	Blinker	***bling**-kèr*
tyre	Reifen	***rye**-fèn*
tyre pressure	Reifendruck	***rye**-fèn-drook*
warning light	Warnlicht	***varn**-likht*
water	Wasser	***vass**-èr*
wheel	Rad	*raht*
windscreen/ windshield	Windschutzscheibe	***vint**-shoots-shye-bè*
wipers	Scheibenwischer	***shye**-bèn-vish-èr*
wrench	Schraubenschlüssel	***shrow**-bèn-shlōō-sèl*

Driving
Accidents & the Police

I'm very sorry, officer	Es tut mir sehr leid *es toot meer zer lite*
I did not see the signal	Ich habe das Signal nicht gesehen *ikh* ***hah****-bè dass zig-****nahl*** *nikht gè-****zay****-èn*
I did not know about that regulation	Ich wußte nichts von dieser Verkehrsregel *ikh* ***voo****-stè nikhts fon* ***dee****-zèr fer-****kerz****-ray-gèl*
I did not understand the sign	Ich wußte nicht, was das Schild bedeutet *ikh* ***voo****-stè nikht vass dass shilt bè-****doy****-tèt*
Here is my driving licence	Hier ist mein Führerschein *heer ist mine* ***fōō****-rèr-shine*
Here is my green card	Hier ist meine grüne Versicherungskarte *heer ist* ***mine****-è* ***grōō****-nè fer-****zikh****-è-roongz-kar-tè*
How much is the fine?	Wie hoch ist das Bußgeld? *vee hōkh ist dass* ***booss****-gelt?*
I haven't got that much. Can I pay at the police station?	Ich habe soviel nicht bei mir. Kann ich auf dem Polizeirevier bezahlen? *ikh* ***hah****-bè* ***zo****-feel nikht bye meer. kan ikh owf daym po-li-****tsye****-re-veer bè-****tsah****-lèn?*
I could not stop in time	Ich konnte nicht mehr rechtzeitig bremsen *ikh* ***kon****-tè nikht mer* ***rekht****-tsye-tikh* ***brem****-zèn*
I was driving at 80 Kmh.	Ich bin mit achtzig Stundenkilometern gefahren *ikh bin mit* ***akh****-tsikh* ***stoon****-dèn-kee-lō-may-tèrn gè-****fah****-rèn*
The car turned without signalling	Das Auto hat, ohne Zeichen zugeben, gewendet *dass* ***ow****-tō hat* ***ō****-nè* ***tsye****-khèn tsoo-****gay****-ben gè-****ven****-dèt*

Driving
Accidents & the Police

He was too close – Er ist zu dicht aufgefahren
*er ist tsoo dikht **owf**-gè-fah-rèn*

I did not see him – Ich habe ihn nicht gesehen
*ikh **hah**-bè een nikht gè-**zay**-èn*

He was driving too fast – Er ist zu schnell gefahren
*er ist tsoo shnel gè-**fah**-rèn*

He did not stop – Er hat nicht angehalten
*er hat nikht **an**-gè-hal-tèn*

He did not give way (yield) – Er hat die Vorfahrt mißachtet
*er hat dee **for**-fart miss-**akh**-tèt*

He stopped very suddenly – Er hat plötzlich gebremst
*er hat **plur'ts**-likh gè-**bremst***

He swerved – Er hat ausgeschert
*er hat **ows**-gè-shert*

He ran into me – Er ist mir hineingefahren
*er ist meer hin-**ine**-gè-fah-rèn*

He overtook on a bend (passed on a curve) – Er hat in einer Kurve überholt
*er hat in **ine**-èr **koor**-vè **ōō**-bèr-hōlt*

His car number (license number) was . . . – Seine Autonummer war . . .
***zine**-è **ow**-tō-noo-mèr var . . .*

The road was wet – Die Straße war naß
*dee **shtrah**-sè var nass*

I skidded – Ich bin ins Schleudern gekommen
*ikh bin ins **shloy**-dèrn gè-**ko**-mèn*

My brakes failed – Meine Bremsen haben versagt
mine**-è **brem**-zèn **hah**-bèn fer-**zahgt

I had a blow-out – Ich hatte eine Reifenpanne
*ikh **ha**-tè **ine**-è **rye**-fèn-pa-nè*

What is your name and address? – Geben Sie mir bitte Ihren Namen und Ihre Adresse
***gay**-bèn zee meer **bit**-è **ee**-rèn **nah**-mèn oont **ee**-rè a-**dress**-è*

We should call the police – Wir sollten die Polizei rufen
*veer **zol**-tèn dee po-li-**tsye** **roo**-fèn*

Hotels

Hotels are officially grouped into categories of 1, 2, 3 or 4 stars. You can also stay at one of the *Raststätten* (primarily for lorry-drivers, but of a good standard), or, especially in country areas, in a *Pension, Hotel Garni*, *Gasthof* or *Gasthaus*. Many places can handle a booking in English, but if you don't want to take any chances . . .

Dear Sirs,
Sehr geehrte Herren,

I wish to stay in Munich from 5/6/85 to 9/6/85
Ich möchte vom 5/6/85 bis zum 9/6/85

- **with my wife**
  mit meiner Frau München besuchen
- **with my family**
  mit meiner Familie München besuchen

Can you provide the following accommodation
Könnten Sie mir folgende Unterkunft besorgen

- **1 single room with shower**
  ein Einzelzimmer mit Dusche
- **1 room with twin beds and bath**
  ein Zimmer mit zwei Einzelbetten und Bad
- **1 room with a double bed**
  ein Doppelzimmer
- **1 double room with a bed for a child**
  ein Doppelzimmer mit einem Kinderbett

and inform me of your inclusive rates for
und mir einige Informationen geben über Inklusivpreise für

- **room and breakfast**
  Übernachtung mit Frühstück
- **room and evening meal**
  Halbpension
- **room and all meals**
  Vollpension

I enclose an International Reply Coupon
In der Anlage finden Sie einen Internationalen Antwortschein

Yours faithfully,
Mit freundlichen Grüßen,

Hotels

You'll have to cope with the reply yourself, but if everything is all right it will mention prices; if it begins '*Wir bedauern, Ihnen mitteilen zu müssen*' you may have problems. If you're checking in on the spot . . .

My name is . . . – Mein Name ist . . .
*mine **nah**-mè ist . . .*

I reserved a room – Ich habe ein Zimmer reserviert
*ikh **hah**-bè ine **tsi**-mèr re-zè-**veert***

Do you have a single room? – Haben Sie ein Einzelzimmer?
***hah**-bèn zee ine **ine**-tsèl-tsi-mèr?*

Do you have a room with twin beds and shower? – Haben Sie ein Zimmer mit zwei Einzelbetten und Dusche?
***hah**-bèn zee ine **tsi**-mèr mit tsvye **ine**-tsèl-be-tèn oont **doo**-shè?*

Do you have a double room with bath? – Haben Sie ein Doppelzimmer mit Bad?
***hah**-bèn zee ine **do**-pèl-tsi-mer mit baht?*

I want to stay for 3 nights – Ich möchte drei Nächte bleiben
*ikh **mur'kh**-tè drye **nekh**-tè **blye**-bèn*

We shall be staying until the sixth of May – Wir bleiben bis sechsten Mai
*veer **blye**-bèn biss **zekh**-stèn mye*

How much is the room per night? – Wieviel kostet das Zimmer pro Nacht?
*vee-**feel kos**-tet dass **tsi**-mèr prō nakht?*

Is that inclusive? – Ist dabei alles inbegriffen?
*ist da-**bye al**-ès **in**-bè-gri-fèn?*

How much is half-board? – Wieviel kostet es mit Halbpension?
*vee-**feel kos**-tèt es mit **halp**-pen-zee-yōn?*

How much is full board? – Wieviel kostet es mit Vollpension?
*vee-**feel kos**-tèt es mit **fol**-pen-zee-yōn?*

Do you have a cot (crib) for our baby? – Haben Sie ein Kinderbett für unser Baby?
***hah**-bèn zee ine **kin**-dèr-bet foor **oon**-zèr **bay**-bee?*

Hotels

What time is –	**breakfast?**
Wann gibt es	Frühstück?
van gipt es	***frōō**-shtōōk?*
–	**lunch?**
	Mittagessen?
	***mi**-tahk-ess-èn?*
–	**dinner?**
	Abendessen?
	***ah**-bènt-ess-èn?*
Can we have breakfast in our room please? –	Können Sie uns bitte das Frühstück aufs Zimmer bringen? *__kur'n__-èn zee oons __bit__-è dass __frōō__-shtōōk owfs __tsi__-mèr __bring__-èn?*
Where can I park the car? –	Wo kann ich das Auto parken? *vō kan ikh dass __ow__-tō __par__-kèn?*
What time does the hotel close? –	Wann macht das Hotel zu? *van makht dass hō-__tel__ tsoo?*
Is there a lift (elevator)? –	Gibt es einen Lift? *gipt es __ine__-èn lift?*
Please call me at 8 o'clock –	Bitte wecken Sie mich um acht Uhr *__bit__-è __ve__-kèn zee mikh oom akht __oo__-èr*
Can I leave these for safe-keeping? –	Könnten Sie das für mich im Safe aufbewahren? *__kur'n__-tèn zee dass fōōr mikh im zayf __owf__-bè-wah-rèn?*
Can I have my things back from the safe? –	Kann ich meine Sachen aus dem Safe wiederhaben? *kan ikh __mine__-è __za__-khèn ows daym zayf __vee__-dèr __hah__-bèn?*
Can I make a telephone call from here? –	Kann ich von hier telefonieren? *kan ikh fon heer tay-lay-fō-__nee__-rèn?*
Is the voltage 220 or 110? –	Ist die Spannung hier zweihundert-zwanzig oder einhundertzehn Volt? *ist dee __shpa__-noong heer __tsvye__-hoon-dèrt-__tsvan__-tsikh ō-dèr __ine__-hoon-dèrt-__tsayn__ volt?*

Hotels

Can I have – **my key please?**
Kann ich bitte meinen Schlüssel haben?
*kan ikh **bit**-è **mine**-èn **shlōō**-sèl **hah**-bèn?*

– **some coat hangers?**
ein paar Kleiderbügel haben?
*ine par **klye**-dèr-bōō-gèl **hah**-bèn?*

– **some notepaper?**
etwas Schreibpapier haben?
***et**-vas **shripe**-pa-peer **hah**-bèn?*

– **an ashtray?**
einen Aschenbecher haben?
***ine**-èn **a**-shèn-be-khèr **hah**-bèn?*

– **another blanket?**
noch eine Decke haben?
*nokh **ine**-è **de**-kè **hah**-bèn?*

– **another pillow?**
noch ein Kissen haben?
*nokh ine **kiss**-èn **hah**-bèn?*

Where is the bathroom? – Wo ist das Badezimmer?
*vō ist dass **bah**-dè-tsi-mèr?*

Where is the socket (outlet) for my razor? – Wo ist die Steckdose für den Rasierapparat?
*vō ist dee **shtek**-dō-zè fōōr dayn ra-**zeer**-a-pa-**raht**?*

There are no towels in the room – Es sind keine Handtücher im Zimmer
*es zint **kine**-è **hant**-tōō-khèr im **tsi**-mèr*

The room is too noisy – Das Zimmer ist zu laut
*dass **tsi**-mèr ist tsoo lowt*

I cannot open the window – Ich bekomme das Fenster nicht auf
*ikh bè-**ko**-mè dass **fen**-stèr nikht owf*

The light is not working – Das Licht geht nicht
dass likht gayt nikht

The air-conditioning is not working – Die Klimaanlage geht nicht
*dee **klee**-ma-an-lah-gè gayt nikht*

The heating is not working – Die Heizung geht nicht
*dee **hye**-tsoong gayt nikht*

Hotels

I cannot turn the heating off – Ich kann die Heizung nicht abdrehen
*ikh kan dee **hye**-tsoong nikht **ap**-dray-èn*

The lock is broken – Das Schloß ist kaputt
*dass shloss ist ka-**poot***

There is no hot water – Es gibt kein heißes Wasser
*es gipt kine **hye**-sès **vass**-er*

The wash basin is dirty – Das Waschbecken ist schmutzig
*dass **vash**-be-kèn ist **shmoot**-tsikh*

There is no plug in the washbasin – Der Stöpsel für das Waschbecken fehlt
*der **shtur'p**-sèl fōōr dass **vash**-be-kèn faylt*

There is no toilet paper – Es ist kein Toilettenpapier da
*es ist kine tō-a-**le**-tèn-pa-peer dah*

Do you have a laundry room? – Haben Sie eine Wäscherei?
***hah**-bèn zee **ine**-è ve-shè-**rye**?*

I want to iron some clothes – Ich möchte ein paar Sachen bügeln
*ikh **mur'kh**-tè ine par **za**-khèn **bōō**-gèln*

I want to stay an extra night – Ich möchte noch eine Nacht bleiben
*ikh **mur'kh**-tè nokh **ine**-è nakht **blye**-bèn*

We will be leaving tomorrow at 9 o'clock – Wir reisen morgen um neun Uhr ab
*veer **rye**-zèn **mor**-gèn oom noyn **oo**-èr ap*

I would like the bill please – Ich hätte gerne die Rechnung, bitte
*ikh **he**-tè **gern**-è dee **rekh**-noong **bit**-è*

Do you accept traveller's cheques? – Nehmen Sie Reiseschecks an?
***nay**-mèn zee **rye**-zè-sheks an?*

Could you have my luggage brought down? – Könnten Sie bitte mein Gepäck herunterbringen lassen
***kur'n**-tèn zee **bit**-è mine gè-**pek** he-**roon**-tèr-bring-èn **lass**-èn?*

Could you order me a taxi? – Könnten Sie mir bitte ein Taxi bestellen?
***kur'n**-tèn zee meer **bit**-è ine **tak**-see bè-**shtel**-èn*

Hotels

Thank you – we enjoyed our stay – Vielen Dank – es hat uns gut gefallen *fee-lèn dank – es hat oons goot gè-**fal**-èn*

If you're a typical absent-minded visitor, you will probably leave something behind when you go home. This letter may help you get it back if you copy it out carefully and insert the name of the missing item after "*ich habe dort*". Of course, you'll have to find out the German word for yourself!

Dear Sirs,
I recently spent some time in your hotel in room 16. I believe I forgot
a pair of shoes
when I left. If you would be good enough to send them on to me I would be most grateful and refund the cost of postage.
Yours faithfully,

Sehr geehrte Herren,
Ich habe vor kurzem einige Tage in Ihrem Hotel verbracht (Zimmer 16). Ich glaube, ich habe dort
ein Paar Schuhe
vergessen. Ich wäre Ihnen sehr dankbar, wenn Sie sie mir schicken könnten. Die Portokosten werde ich selbstverständlich ersetzen.
Mit freundlichen Grüßen,

Rented Villas

This kind of holiday is increasingly popular, so we hope this section will help you settle into your home from home.

We have arranged to rent a house – Wir haben ein Haus gemietet
veer ***hah****-bèn ine hows gè-****mee****-tèt*

Here is our booking – Hier ist unsere Buchung
heer ist ***oon****-zè-rè* ***bookh****-oong*

We need two sets of keys – Wir brauchen zwei Schlüsselsätze
veer ***brow****-khèn tsvye* ***shlōō****-sèl-zayts-è*

Will you show us around? – Würden Sie uns herumführen?
vōōr*-dèn zee oons he-****room****-fōō-rèn?*

Which is the key for this door? – Welcher Schlüssel ist für diese Tür?
vel*-khèr* ***shlōō****-sèl ist fōōr* ***dee****-zè tōōr?*

Where are the fuses? – Wo sind die Sicherungen?
vō zint dee ***zikh****-è-roong-èn?*

Where is the water heater? – Wo ist der Wasserboiler?
vō ist der ***vass****-er-boy-lèr?*

Please show us how this works – Bitte zeigen Sie uns, wie das funktioniert
bit*-è* ***tsye****-gèn zee oons vee dass foonk-tsee-ō-****neert***

How does the heating work? – Wie funktioniert die Heizung?
*vee foonk-tsee-ō-****neert*** *dee* ***hye****-tsoong?*

When does the help come? – Wann kommt die Zugehfrau?
*van komt dee tsoo-****gay****-frow?*

Is there any spare bedding? – Gibt es noch Extra-Bettzeug?
gipt es nokh ***eks****-tra-****bet****-tsoyg?*

Can I contact you if there are any problems? – Kann ich mich an Sie wenden, wenn es Probleme gibt?
kan ikh mikh an zee ***ven****-dèn ven es pro-****blay****-mè gipt?*

The cooker (stove) does not work – Der Herd funktioniert nicht
*der hert foonk-tsee-ō-****neert*** *nikht*

I can't open the windows – Ich bekomme die Fenster nicht auf
*ikh bè-****ko****-mè dee* ***fen****-stèr nikht owf*

Rented Villas

We can't get any water – Es kommt kein Wasser
es komt kine ***vass****-er*

The toilet won't flush – Die Spülung geht nicht
dee ***shpōō****-loong gayt nikht*

A fuse has blown – Eine Sicherung ist durchgebrannt
ine*-è* ***zikh****-è-roong ist* ***doorkh****-gè-brant*

There is a gas leak – Die Gasleitung ist undicht
dee ***gahs****-lye-toong ist* ***oon****-dikht*

I need somebody to fix this – Ich brauche jemanden, der das reparieren kann
ikh ***brow****-khè* ***yay****-man-dèn der dass re-pa-****ree****-rèn kan*

bath	Bad *baht*	**mirror**	Spiegel ***shpee****-gèl*
bathroom	Badezimmer ***bah****-dè-tsi-mèr*	**pan**	Pfanne ***pfa****-nè*
bed	Bett *bet*	**plate**	Teller ***te****-lèr*
brush	Bürste ***bōōr****-stè*	**refrigerator**	Kühlschrank ***kōōl****-shrank*
can opener	Dosenöffner ***dō****-zèn-ur'f-nèr*	**sheet**	Bettlaken ***bet****-la-kèn*
chair	Stuhl *shtool*	**sink**	Spülbecken ***shpōōl****-be-kèn*
cooker	Herd *hert*	**spoon**	Löffel ***lur'****-fèl*
corkscrew	Korkenzieher ***kor****-kèn-tsee-èr*	**stove**	Herd *hert*
cup	Tasse ***tass****-è*	**table**	Tisch *tish*
fork	Gabel ***gah****-bèl*	**tap**	Wasserhahn ***vass****-er-hahn*
glass	Glas *glass*	**toilet**	Toilette *tō-a-****le****-tè*
kitchen	Küche ***kōō****-khè*	**vacuum cleaner**	Staubsauger ***shtowb****-sow-gèr*
knife	Messer ***mess****-èr*	**washbasin**	Waschbecken ***vash****-be-kèn*

Travelling with a Family

If you take the children – *die Kinder* – away with you, anything can happen and probably will, but these phrases should be useful in at least some of the situations you'll encounter.

There are four of us – Wir sind zu viert
veer zint tsoo feert

my wife – meine Frau
***mine**-è frow*

my husband – mein Mann
mine man

my daughter – meine Tochter
***mine**-è **tokh**-tèr*

my son – mein Sohn
mine zōn

Have you got a cot (crib) for our baby? – Haben Sie ein Kinderbett für unser Baby?
***hah**-bèn zee ine **kin**-dèr-bet fōōr **oon**-zèr **bay**-bee?*

Can my son sleep in our room? – Kann mein Sohn bei uns im Zimmer schlafen?
*kan mine zōn bye oons im **tsi**-mèr **shlah**-fèn?*

Are there any other children in the hotel? – Sind im Hotel noch mehr Kinder?
*zint im hō-**tel** nokh mer **kin**-dèr?*

How old are your children? – Wie alt sind Ihre Kinder?
*vee alt zint **ee**-rè **kin**-dèr?*

The boy is 9 years old – Der Junge ist neun Jahre alt
*der **yoong**-è ist noyn **yah**-rè alt*

The girl is 15 months – Das Mädchen ist fünfzehn Monate alt
*das **mayt**-khèn ist **fōōnf**-tsayn **mō**-na-tè alt*

Where can I feed my baby? – Wo kann ich mein Baby füttern?
*vō kan ikh mine **bay**-bee **fōō**-tèrn?*

Have you got a highchair? – Haben Sie einen Kinderstuhl?
***hah**-bèn zee **ine**-èn **kin**-dèr-shtool?*

Travelling with a Family

Can you warm this bottle for me? – Können Sie diese Flasche für mich wärmen?
kur'n-èn zee dee-zè flash-è fōōr mikh ver-mèn?

I need some disposable nappies (diapers) – Ich brauche ein paar Papierwindeln
ikh brow-khè ine par pa-peer-vin-dèln

Do you know anyone who will babysit for us? – Kennen Sie jemanden, der für uns babysitten kann?
ken-èn zee yay-man-dèn der fōōr oons bay-bee-zi-tèn kan?

We will be back at 11 – Wir werden um elf Uhr zurück sein
veer ver-dèn oom elf oo-èr tsoo-rōōk zine

She goes to bed at 8 – Sie geht um acht Uhr ins Bett
zee gayt oom akht oo-èr ins bet

Are there any organized activities for the children? – Gibt es irgendwelche Freizeitveranstaltungen für Kinder?
gipt es eer-gènt-vel-khè frye-tsite-fer-an-shtal-toong-èn fōōr kin-dèr?

Is there a paddling pool? – Gibt es hier ein Planschbecken?
gipt es heer ine plansh-be-kèn?

Is there an amusement park? – Gibt es hier einen Vergnügungspark?
gipt es heer ine-èn fer-gnōō-goongz-park?

Is there a zoo nearby? – Gibt es hier in der Nähe einen Zoo?
gipt es heer in der nay-è ine-èn tsō?

My son has hurt himself – Mein Sohn hat sich wehgetan
mine zōn hat zikh vay-gè-tahn

My daughter is ill – Meine Tochter ist krank
mine-è tokh-tèr ist krank

I'm very sorry. That was very naughty of him/her – Es tut mir leid – das war sehr ungezogen von ihm/ihr
es toot meer lite – dass var zer oon-gè-tsō-gèn fon eem/eer

Camping

Is there anywhere for us to camp near here? – Können wir irgendwo hier in der Nähe zelten?
__kur'n__-èn veer __eer__-gènt-vō heer in der __nay__-è __tsel__-tèn?

Have you a site for our tent? – Haben Sie einen Zeltplatz für uns?
__hah__-bèn zee __ine__-èn __tselt__-plats fōōr oons?

Do you mind if we camp on your land? – Haben Sie etwas dagegen, wenn wir auf Ihrem Grundstück zelten?
__hah__-bèn zee __et__-vas da-__gay__-gèn ven veer owf __ee__-rèm __groont__-shtōōk __tsel__-tèn?

May we pitch our tent here? – Dürfen wir unser Zelt hier aufschlagen?
__dōōr__-fèn veer __oon__-zèr tselt heer __owf__-shlah-gèn?

This site is very muddy – Der Platz ist sehr schlammig
der plats ist zer __shla__-mikh

Could we have a more sheltered site? – Könnten wir eine besser geschützte Stelle haben?
__kur'n__-tèn veer __ine__-è __be__-sèr gè-__shōōts__-tè __shte__-lè __hah__-bèn?

Can we put our caravan (trailer) here? – Können wir unseren Wohnwagen hier hinstellen?
__kur'n__-èn veer __oon__-zè-rèn __vōn__-vah-gèn heer __hin__-shte-lèn?

Is there a shop on the site? – Gibt es einen Laden auf dem Campingplatz?
gipt es __ine__-èn __lah__-dèn owf daym __kam__-ping-plats?

Can I have a shower? – Kann ich duschen?
kan ikh __doo__-shèn?

Where is the drinking water? – Wo gibt es Trinkwasser?
vō gipt es __trink__-vass-er?

Where are the toilets and washroom? – Wo sind die Toiletten und der Waschraum?
vō zint dee tō-a-__le__-tèn oont der __vash__-rowm?

Camping Equipment

Where can we wash our dishes? – Wo können wir abwaschen?
*vō **kur'n**-èn veer **ap**-vash-èn?*

Is there another camp-site near here? – Gibt es hier in der Nähe noch einen anderen Campingplatz?
*gipt es heer in der **nay**-è nokh **ine**-èn **an**-dè-rèn **kam**-ping-plats?*

air-mattress	Luftmatratze *looft-ma-tra-tsè*	**guy line**	Zeltschnur *tselt-shnoor*
back pack	Rucksack *rook-zak*	**knife**	Messer *mess-èr*
bottle opener	Flaschenöffner *flash-èn-ur'f-nèr*	**mallet**	Holzhammer *holts-ha-mèr*
bucket	Eimer *eye-mèr*	**matches**	Streichhölzer *shtrye-khur'l-tsèr*
camp bed	Campingliege *kam-ping-lee-gè*	**pail**	Eimer *eye-mèr*
camp chair	Campingstuhl *kam-ping-shtool*	**penknife**	Taschenmesser *tash-èn-mess-èr*
candle	Kerze *ker-tsè*	**plate**	Teller *te-lèr*
can opener	Dosenöffner *dō-zèn-ur'f-nèr*	**rucksack**	Rucksack *rook-zak*
cup	Tasse *tass-è*	**shelter**	Unterstand *oon-tèr-shtant*
fire	Feuer *foy-èr*	**sleeping bag**	Schlafsack *shlahf-zak*
flashlight	Taschenlampe *tash-èn-lam-pè*	**spoon**	Löffel *lur'-fèl*
fly sheet	Überzelt *ōō-bèr-tselt*	**stove**	Kocher *kokh-èr*
folding table	Klapptisch *klap-tish*	**tent**	Zelt *tselt*
fork	Gabel *gah-bèl*	**tent peg**	Hering *hay-ring*
frying pan	Bratpfanne *braht-pfa-nè*	**tent pole**	Zeltstange *tselt-shtang-è*
ground	Boden *bō-dèn*	**thermos flask**	Thermosflasche *ter-mōs-flash-è*
ground sheet	Bodenplane *bō-dèn-plah-nè*	**torch**	Taschenlampe *tash-èn-lam-pè*

Youth Hostels

Here is my international membership card – Hier ist mein internationaler Jugendherbergsausweis
*heer ist mine in-ter-nat-see-ō-**nah**-ler **yoo**-gènt-her-berks-**ows**-vice*

How long can I stay? – Wie lange kann ich hier bleiben?
*vee **lang**-è kan ikh heer **blye**-bèn?*

I want to stay two nights here – Ich möchte zwei Nächte hier bleiben
*ikh **mur'kh**-tè tsvye **nekh**-tè heer **blye**-bèn*

I would like to join here – Ich möchte gerne Mitglied werden
*ikh **mur'kh**-tè **gern**-è **mit**-gleet **ver**-dèn*

Are you open during the day? – Ist die Herberge tagsüber offen?
*ist dee **her**-ber-gè **tahgs**-ōō-ber **o**-fèn?*

What time do you close? – Um wieviel Uhr machen Sie zu?
*oom **vee**-feel **oo**-èr **makh**-èn zee tsoo?*

Do you serve meals? – Bekommt man hier etwas zu essen?
*bè-**komt** man heer **et**-vass tsoo **ess**-èn?*

Can I use the kitchen? – Kann ich hier selbst kochen?
*Kan ikh heer **zelpst kokh**-èn?*

I want to rent a sheet-sleeping bag – Ich möchte einen Leinenschlafsack ausleihen
*ikh **mur'kh**-tè **ine**-èn **line**-èn-shlahf-zak **ows**-lye-èn*

Is there another youth hostel near here? – Gibt es hier in der Nähe noch eine Jugendherberge?
*gipt es heer in der **nay**-è nokh **ine**-è **yoo**-gènt-**her**-berg-è?*

Churches

Where is there – **a Catholic church?**
Wo gibt es eine katholische Kirche?
vo gipt es ***ine****-è ka-****tō****-lish-è* ***keer****-khè?*

– **a Protestant church?**
eine protestantische Kirche?
ine*-è pro-tes-****tant****-ish-è* ***keer****-khè?*

– **a Baptist church?**
eine Baptistenkirche?
ine*-è bap-****tis****-tèn* ***keer****-khè?*

– **a Synagogue?**
eine Synagoge?
ine*-è zōō-na-****gog****-è?*

– **a Mosque?**
eine Moschee?
ine*-è mo-****shay****?*

What time is the service? – Um wieviel Uhr ist der Gottesdienst?
oom ***vee****-feel* ***oo****-èr ist der* ***go****-tes-deenst?*

I'd like to see – **a priest**
Ich möchte mit einem Priester sprechen
ikh ***mur'kh****-tè mit* ***ine****-èm* ***pree****-ster* ***shpre****-khèn*

– **a minister**
einem protestantischen Pfarrer sprechen
ine*-èm pro-tes-****tant****-ish-èn* ***pfa****-rer* ***shpre****-khèn*

– **a rabbi**
einem Rabbi sprechen
ine*-èm* ***ra****-bi* ***shpre****-khèn*

. . . who speaks English – . . . der Englisch spricht
. . . der ***eng****-lish shprikht*

What will the choir be singing? – Was wird der Chor singen?
vass veert der kor ***zing****-èn?*

The Weather

You may need to know the weather forecast, or you may just want to make conversation . . .

It's a lovely day, isn't it? – Schönes Wetter heute, nicht wahr?
__shur'__nès __ve__-ter __hoy__-tè, nikht var?

It's too hot for me – Es ist mir zu heiß
es ist meer tsoo hice

There's a nice breeze – Es weht ein angenehmer Wind
es vayt ine __an__-gè-nay-mer vint

It's raining – Es regnet
es __rayg__-nèt

It's windy – Es ist windig
es ist __vin__-dikh

It's snowing – Es schneit
es shnite

It's foggy – Es ist neblig
es ist __nay__-blikh

It's cold – Es ist kalt
es ist kalt

Is it going – **to be fine?**
Wird es schön sein?
veert es shur'n zine?

– **to rain?**
regnen?
__rayg__-nèn?

– **to be windy?**
windig sein?
__vin__-dikh zine?

– **to snow?**
schneien?
__shnye__-èn?

What is the temperature? – Wieviel Grad hat es?
__vee__-feel graht hat es?

Is it going to stay like this? – Wird es so bleiben?
veert es zō __blye__-bèn?

The Weather

Will the weather improve? – Wird das Wetter besser werden?
*veert dass **ve**-ter **be**-ser **ver**-dèn?*

Is it going to get any cooler? – Wird es kälter werden?
*veert es **kel**-ter **ver**-dèn?*

Will the wind go down? – Wird sich der Wind legen?
*veert zikh der vint **lay**-gèn?*

Is there going to be a thunderstorm? – Wird es ein Gewitter geben?
*veert es ine gè-**vi**-ter **gay**-bèn?*

Is the sea calm? – Ist das Meer ruhig?
*ist dass **may**-èr **roo**-ikh?*

Is the water warm? – Ist das Wasser warm?
*ist dass **vass**-er varm?*

When is high tide? – Wann kommt die Flut?
van komt dee floot?

It's a clear night – Es ist eine klare Nacht
*es ist **ine**-è **klah**-rè nakht*

Will it be cold tonight? – Wird es heute nacht kalt werden?
*veert es **hoy**-tè nakht kalt **ver**-dèn?*

The stars are out – Es ist eine sternenklare Nacht
*es ist **ine**-è **stern**-èn-klah-rè nakht*

Leisure & Entertainment
On the Beach

You may see a coloured flag on the beach. If it's red, don't go swimming – it's not safe and there's no lifeguard. If the flag's orange, it's still unsafe, but there is a lifeguard around. The green flag means that you can go right ahead!

Is it safe to swim here? – Kann man hier schwimmen?
*kan man heer **shvim**-èn?*

Is this a private beach? – Ist dies ein Privatstrand?
*ist dees ine pree-**vaht**-shtrant?*

Can you recommend a quiet beach? – Können Sie mir einen ruhigen Strand empfehlen?
***kur'n**-èn zee meer **ine**-èn **roo**-ikh-èn shtrant em-**pfay**-lèn?*

Where can we change? – Wo können wir uns umziehen?
*vō **kur'n**-èn veer oons **oom**-tsee-èn?*

Can I rent – **a deck chair?**
Kann ich einen Liegestuhl mieten?
*kan ikh **ine**-èn **lee**-gè-shtool **mee**-tèn?*

– **a sunshade?**
einen Sonnenschirm mieten?
***ine**-èn **zo**-nèn-shirm **mee**-tèn?*

– **a sailing boat?**
ein Segelboot mieten?
*ine **zay**-gèl-bōt **mee**-tèn?*

Is it possible to go – **sailing?**
Kann man hier segeln?
*kan man heer **zay**-gèln?*

– **water ski-ing?**
Wasserski fahren?
***vass**-er-shee **fah**-rèn?*

– **surfing?**
surfen?
***zoor**-fèn?*

– **wind surfing?**
windsurfen?
***vint**-zoor-fèn?*

Leisure & Entertainment
Outdoors & Night Life

Is there a swimming pool? – Ist hier ein Freibad?
*ist heer ine **frye**-baht?*

Is there somewhere I can – **play tennis?**
Kann ich hier irgendwo Tennis spielen?
*kan ikh heer **eer**-gènt-vō **te**-niss **shpeel**-èn?*
– **play golf?**
Golf spielen?
*golf **shpeel**-èn?*

Is it possible to go riding? – Kann man hier reiten?
*kan man heer **rye**-tèn?*

Can I go fishing? – Kann ich hier angeln gehen?
*kan ikh heer **ang**-èln **gay**-èn?*

Can I rent the equipment? – Kann ich die Ausrüstung leihen?
*kan ikh dee **ows**-rōōs-toong **lye**-èn?*

Do you know any interesting walks? – Kennen Sie irgendwelche interessante Wanderwege?
*__ken__-èn zee **eer**-gènt-vel-khè in-tè-re-**san**-tè **van**-dèr-vay-gè?*

Are there any local festivals nearby? – Gibt es hier in der Nähe irgendwelche Volksfeste?
*gipt es heer in der **nay**-è **eer**-gènt-vel-khè **folks**-fes-tè?*

Are there any films in English? – Laufen hier Filme auf englisch?
*__low__-fèn heer **fil**-mè owf **eng**-lish?*

Is there a concert? – Gibt es ein Konzert?
*gipt es ine kon-**tsert**?*

Two balcony tickets, please – Zweimal erster Rang, bitte
*__tsvye__-mal **erst**-èr rang, **bit**-è*

Two stalls (orchestra) tickets, please – Zweimal Sperrsitz, bitte
*__tsvye__-mal **shper**-zits, **bit**-è*

Are there any good night-clubs? – Gibt es hier gute Nachtclubs?
*gipt es heer **goo**-tè **nakht**-klubz?*

Is there a disco? – Gibt es hier eine Diskothek?
*gipt es heer **ine**-è dis-kō-**tayk**?*

Sightseeing

What is there to see here? –	Was gibt es hier zu sehen? *vass gipt es heer tsoo* ***zay****-èn?*
Have you got a town guide? –	Haben Sie einen Fremdenführer? ***hah****-bèn zee* ***ine****-èn* ***frem****-dèn-fōō-rèr?*
What is this building? –	Was für ein Gebäude ist das? *vass fōōr ine gè-****boy****-dè ist dass?*
When was it built? –	Wann wurde es erbaut? *van voor-dè es er-****bowt****?*
Is it open to the public? –	Kann man es besichtigen? *kan man es bè-****zikh****-ti-gèn?*
Are there any sight-seeing tours? –	Gibt es hier Besichtigungsfahrten? *gipt es heer bè-****sikh****-ti-goongs-fahr-tèn?*
Is there a tour of the castle? –	Gibt es eine Führung durch das Schloß? *gipt es* ***ine****-è* ***fōō****-roong doorkh dass shloss?*
When is the bus tour of the town? –	Wann ist die Stadtrundfahrt? *van ist dee* ***shtat****-roont-fart?*
How long does the tour take? –	Wie lange dauert die Rundfahrt? *vee* ***lang****-è* ***dow****-ert dee* ***roont****-fart?*
Are there any boat trips on the river? –	Gibt es Ausflugsfahrten auf dem Fluß? *gipt es* ***ows****-flooks-far-tèn owf daym flooss?*
Are there any guided tours of the cathedral? –	Gibt es eine Führung durch die Kathedrale? *gipt es* ***ine****-è* ***fōō****-roong doorkh dee ka-tay-****drah****-lè?*
Is there an English-speaking guide? –	Ist hier ein Fremdenführer, der englisch spricht? *ist heer ine* ***frem****-dèn-fōō-rèr der* ***eng****-lish shprikht?*
Have you got an English guidebook? –	Haben Sie einen englischen Fremdenführer? ***hah****-bèn zee* ***ine****-èn* ***eng****-lish-èn* ***frem****-dèn-fōō-rèr?*

Sightseeing

What time does the museum open? –	Wann öffnet das Museum? *van* ***ur'f****-nèt dass moo-****zay****-oom?*
Can we go in? –	Können wir eintreten? ***kur'n****-èn veer* ***ine****-tray-tèn?*
Are these monuments illuminated at night? –	Werden diese Denkmäler abends beleuchtet? ***ver****-dèn* ***dee****-zè* ***dengk****-may-lèr* ***ah****-bènts bè-****loykh****-tèt?*
What is the admission charge? –	Wieviel kostet der Eintritt? ***vee****-feel* ***kos****-tèt der* ***ine****-trit?*
Can we go up to the top? –	Können wir bis nach oben gehen? ***kur'n****-èn veer biss nahkh ō-bèn* ***gay****-èn?*
Where is the best view? –	Von wo hat man die beste Aussicht? *fon vō hat man dee* ***best****-è* ***ows****-zikht?*
Can I take photos? –	Kann ich fotografieren? *kan ikh fō-tō-gra-****fee****-rèn?*
Can I use a flash? –	Kann ich ein Blitzlicht benutzen? *kan ikh ine* ***blits****-likht bè-****noots****-èn?*
Have you got any postcards? –	Haben Sie Postkarten? ***hah****-bèn zee* ***post****-kar-tèn?*
Have you got any colour slides? –	Haben Sie Farbdias? ***hah****-bèn zee* ***farp****-dee-as?*
Where can you buy souvenirs? –	Wo kann ich Andenken kaufen? *vo kan ikh* ***an****-deng-kèn* ***kow****-fèn?*
Would you take a photo of us please? –	Würden Sie bitte ein Bild von uns machen? ***vōōr****-dèn zee* ***bit****-è ine bilt fon oons* ***makh****-èn?*

Eating & Drinking
Restaurants

Eating out in Germany can be a memorable experience. In cities you will find international-style restaurants, but most Germans prefer those traditional establishments, the *Wirtshaus* and the *Gasthof*, where you will find authentic local cooking. Try to avoid places obviously catering for tourists, where standards are not likely to be high for customers who are only passing through. The best recommendation is the presence of the Germans themselves. The menu reader on page 64 will help you decide what to eat – don't miss the opportunity to sample local specialities.

Can we have a table for two? – Können wir einen Tisch für zwei Personen haben?
kur'n-èn veer ***ine****-èn tish fo͞or tsvye per-***zō****-nèn* ***hah****-bèn?*

Can I book a table for four at 8 o'clock? – Kann ich für acht Uhr einen Tisch für vier Personen bestellen?
kan ikh fo͞or akht ***oo****-èr* ***ine****-èn tish fo͞or feer per-***zō****-nèn bè-shtel-èn?*

We'd like a table – **by the window**
Wir hätten gerne einen Tisch – am Fenster
veer ***he****-tèn* ***gern****-è* ***ine****-èn tish* – *am* ***fen****-stèr*

– **on the terrace**
auf der Terrasse
*owf der te-***rass****-è*

The menu please – Die Speisekarte, bitte!
dee ***shpye****-zè-kar-tè* ***bit****-è*

Do you have a set menu? – Gibt es ein Tagesmenü?
gipt es ine ***tah****-gès-mè-no͞o?*

I will take the set menu – Ich nehme das Tagesmenü
ikh ***nay****-mè dass* ***tah****-gès-mè-no͞o*

We will take the menu at 15 Deutschmarks – Wir hätten gerne das Menü zu fünfzehn Mark
veer ***he****-tèn* ***gern****-è dass mè-***no͞o*** *tsoo* ***fo͞onf****-tsayn mark*

Is this good? – Können Sie das empfehlen?
kur'n*-èn zee dass em-***pfay****-lèn?*

Eating & Drinking

Restaurants

What is this dish like? – Was für ein Gericht ist das?
*vass fo͞or ine gè-**rikht** ist dass?*

What do you recommend? – Was empfehlen Sie?
*vass em-**pfay**-lèn zee?*

Do you have a local speciality? – Haben Sie eine Spezialität dieser Gegend?
***hah**-bèn zee **ine**-è shpay-tsee-a-li-**tayt** **dee**-zer **gay**-gènt?*

I'll take that – Ich nehme das
*ikh **nay**-mè dass*

We will begin with onion soup – Als Vorspeise hätten wir gerne Zwiebelsuppe
*als **for**-shpye-zè **het**-èn veer **gern**-è **tsvee**-bèl-zoo-pè*

I will have steak and chips – Ich hätte gerne Steak und Pommes frites
*ikh **het**-è **gern**-è shtayk oont pom frit*

I like it – **very rare**
Ich hätte es gerne – blutig
*ikh **het**-è es **gern**-è* – ***bloo**-tikh*

– **rare**
rot
rōt

– **medium rare**
halbgebraten
***halp**-gè-brah-tèn*

– **well done**
durchgebraten
***doorkh**-gè-brah-tèn*

Are vegetables included? – Ist Gemüse dabei?
*ist gè-**mo͞o**-zè da-**bye**?*

Is this cheese very strong? – Ist dieser Käse sehr scharf?
*ist **dee**-zer **kay**-zè zer sharf?*

That is for me – Das ist für mich
dass ist fo͞or mikh

Eating & Drinking
Restaurants

That is for over here – Das kommt hierhin
*dass komt **heer**-hin*

How do I eat this? – Wie wird das gegessen?
*vee veert dass gè-**gess**-èn?*

Could we have some more bread please? – Könnten wir bitte noch etwas Brot haben?
***kur'n**-tèn veer **bit**-è nokh **et**-vas brōt **hah**-bèn?*

Could I have some butter? – Kann ich bitte etwas Butter haben?
*kan ikh **bit**-è **et**-vas **boo**-tèr **hah**-bèn?*

What is this called? – Wie heißt das?
vee hye-st dass?

Would you bring another glass please? – Würden Sie bitte noch ein Glas bringen?
***vōōr**-dèn zee **bit**-è nokh ine glass **bring**-èn?*

That is not what I ordered – Das habe ich nicht bestellt
*dass **hah**-bè ikh nikht bè-**shtelt***

This is very salty – Das ist sehr salzig
*dass ist zer **zal**-tsikh*

I wanted cheese – Ich hatte Käse bestellt
*ikh **ha**-tè **kay**-zè bè-**shtelt***

Have you forgotten the soup – Haben Sie die Suppe vergessen?
***hah**-bèn zee dee **zoo**-pè fer-**gess**-èn?*

This is cold – Das ist kalt
dass ist kalt

This is very good – Es schmeckt sehr gut
es shmekt zer goot

I'll have a dessert please – Ich hätte gerne ein Dessert
*ikh **het**-è **gern**-è ine **de**-ser*

The wine list please – Die Weinliste, bitte
*dee **vine**-lis-tè, **bit**-è*

Eating & Drinking
Restaurants

Which wine do you recommend? –	Welchen Wein können Sie mir empfehlen? *vel-khèn vine **kur'n**-èn zee meer em-**pfay**-lèn?*
Is the local wine good? –	Schmeckt der Wein aus dieser Gegend gut? *shmekt der vine ows **dee**-zer **gay**-gènt goot?*
We'll take the Riesling –	Wir nehmen den Riesling *veer **nay**-mèn dayn **rees**-ling*
A small carafe of red wine, please –	Eine kleine Karaffe Rotwein, bitte ***ine**-è **kline**-è ka-**raf**-è **rōt**-vine, **bit**-è*
A glass (¼ litre) of white wine, please –	Ein Viertel Weißwein, bitte *ine **feer**-tèl **vice**-vine, **bit**-è*
Another bottle, please –	Noch eine Flasche, bitte *nokh **ine**-è **flash**-è, **bit**-è*
Some plain water, please –	Ein Glas Wasser, bitte *ine glass **vass**-er, **bit**-è*
A beer, please –	Ein Bier, bitte *ine beer, **bit**-è*
Black coffee, please –	Einen Kaffee, bitte ***ine**-èn **ka**-fay, **bit**-è*
Coffee with milk, please –	Einen Milchkaffee, bitte ***ine**-èn **milkh**-ka-fay, **bit**-è*
The bill, please –	Die Rechnung, bitte! *dee **rekh**-noong, **bit**-è*
Is service included? –	Ist Bedienung inbegriffen? *ist bè-**dee**-noong **in**-bè-gri-fèn?*
The meal was excellent –	Das Essen war ausgezeichnet *dass **ess**-èn var **ows**-gè-tsye-khnèt*

Eating & Drinking
Menu Reader

We hope that this menu reader will show how varied and appealing German cooking can be, and enable you to choose your meal with confidence.

Aalsuppe
Eel soup

Aal Grün mit Dillsauce
Fresh eel with dill sauce

Achleitner
Sharp and appetizing cheese (Austria)

Aufgebackene Spätzli
Fried dumplings served with an egg sauce (Switzerland)

Ballen
Dish baked with herbs (Switzerland)

Bauernfrühstück
Scrambled eggs, bacon, cooked diced potatoes, onions, tomatoes

Bauernschmaus
Assortment of roast and smoked pork; sausages, sauerkraut and dumplings (Austria)

Bayerisches Kraut
Shredded cabbage cooked with sliced apples, wine and sugar

Biersuppe
Beer soup flavoured with cinnamon and lemon

Bismarckheringe
Herring fillets marinated in a vinegary sauce

Bohnensalat
Bean salad

Bohnensuppe
Thick brown bean soup with small pieces of smoked bacon (esp. Austria)

Bouillon/Fleischbrühe
Clear soup/broth

Brathähnchen
Roast chicken

Bratheringe
Fresh fried herring marinated in a vinegar, herb and onion dressing

Bratkartoffeln
Fried potatoes

Bündnerfleisch
Raw beef, smoked and dried, served thinly sliced (Switzerland)

Dampfnudel
Yeast dumpling

Deutsche Beefsteaks/Bouletten/Frikadellen
Fried, flat minced meat balls

Edamer
A German version of the Dutch cheese. Mild flavour

Eierkuchen
Pancakes

Eisbein
Pickled knuckle of pork

Eating & Drinking
Menu Reader

Emmentaler
Hard cheese produced from whole milk, with fairly large holes (Switzerland)

Emmentaler Schnitzel
Fried veal escalopes with *Emmentaler* cheese slices fried on each side of the meat (Switzerland)

Erbsenpüree
Dried green pea purée

Erdäpfelknödel
Potato and semolina dumplings (Austria)

Erdäpfelnudeln
Fried, boiled potato balls tossed in fried breadcrumbs (Austria)

Falscher Hase
Baked minced meat loaf

Fischauflauf
Fish pudding (Austria)

Fischsuppe
Fish soup

Forelle blau
Trout

Forelle mit Genfersauce
Trout, cooked in white wine and lemon juice, covered with a milk and egg yolk sauce (Switzerland)

Forelle Steiermark
Small filleted trout, larded with bacon strips, served with a white sauce (Austria)

Hühnerfrikassée
Chicken fricassee

Hasenpfeffer
Jugged hare

Gebratene Ente
Roast duck

Gebackenes Goldbarschfilet
Fried golden perch fillet in egg and breadcrumbs

Gefüllte Kalbsbrust
Roast stuffed breast of veal

Gegrillter Lachs
Grilled salmon

Gemischter Salat
Mixed salad

Gemüseplatte
Assorted vegetables

Geräucherter Aal
Smoked eel

Geschnetzeltes Kalbfleisch
Thinly sliced veal with a thick cream sauce (Switzerland)

Gitziprägel
Baked rabbit in batter (Switzerland)

Grießklößchen
Semolina dumplings

Grießnockerlnsuppe
Beef broth with chives, served with semolina dumplings (Austria)

Grünkernsuppe
Green corn and cream soup

Grüner Salat
Lettuce mixed with a dressing of vinegar and oil

Eating & Drinking
Menu Reader

Güggeli/Mistchratzerli
Roast chicken with onions and mushrooms in a white wine sauce (Switzerland)

Gulasch
Highly seasoned stew, flavoured with paprika

Gulaschsuppe
Thick, spicy meat soup, flavoured with paprika

Gurkensalat
Cucumber salad

Huhn mit Käsesauce
Boiled chicken with cheese sauce (Switzerland)

Jägergulasch
Venison stew with bacon, ham, juniper berries and sour cream, flavoured with paprika (Austria)

Jura Omelette
Emmentaler cheese, bacon, tomato, onion and potato omelette (Switzerland)

Junges Gemüse
Young vegetables

Kaiserfleisch
Boiled, smoked pork (Austria)

Kalbsbraten
Roast veal

Kalbsnierenbraten
Roast loin of veal including the kidneys

Karpfen in Bier
Carp poached in beer, red wine and onion, flavoured with bay leaf, lemon peel and peppercorns (Austria)

Kartoffelklöße
Potato dumplings

Kartoffelpfluten
Potato dumplings served with fried onion rings (Switzerland)

Kartoffelpitte
Baked potatoes, dried pears, milk and diced bacon (Switzerland)

Kartoffelpüree/Kartoffelbrei
Mashed potatoes

Käsefondue
Usually made with a mixture of *Gruyère* and *Emmentaler* cheese, melted with white wine and Kirsch. Bits of bread are dipped into the hot mixture and eaten straight from the fondue dish (Switzerland)

Käsesalat
Cheese salad (Switzerland)

Käsesuppe
Cheese soup (Switzerland)

Kasseler Rippenspeer
Pickled, smoked saddle of pork

Kloß
Dumpling

Knödel
Dumpling (Austria)

Kohlroulade
Cabbage stuffed with a minced meat mixture and baked in the oven (Austria)

Königsberger Kloß
Meatballs, served in a thick white sauce with capers in it

Kopfsalat
see Grüner Salat

Krautsalat
Cabbage salad flavoured with caraway seeds

Kümmelbraten
Caraway-flavoured roast beef (Austria)

Labskaus
Traditional sailors' dish consisting of cured pork, herring and potatoes, and highly flavoured. Eaten with fried eggs, *Matjesfilets*, and picked vegetables.

Leberkäs
Pork liver meat loaf

Leberknödel
Liver dumplings

Leberknödelsuppe
Beef soup with small liver dumplings (Austria)

Leberspätzle
Liver dumplings

Leipziger Allerlei
A mixture of green peas, carrots, cauliflower and cabbage

Limburger
Strong cheese flavoured with herbs

Liptauer
Cream cheese with paprika and herbs (Austria)

Maluns
Sliced and grated potato mixture fried in lard (Switzerland)

Markklößchen
Small beef-marrow dumplings

Matjesfilets
Soused herring fillets in a thick sauce

Maultasche
Small *ravioli*-like pasta bags filled with a special pork, veal and spinach mixture

Münster
Strong cheese with caraway seeds

Nockerl
Small dumplings (Austria)

Nudeln
Noodles

Omelette mit Pilzen
Mushroom omelette

Ochsenschwanzsuppe
Oxtail soup

Paprikahähnchen
Chicken stewed with onions and flavoured with paprika

Pfannkuchen
Pancakes

Pommes frites
Chips (French fries)

Quark
Curd cheese

Raclette
Fried cheese scraped onto a warm plate after having been melted (Switzerland)

Räucherlachs
Smoked salmon

Eating & Drinking
Menu Reader

Rehrücken
Roast saddle of venison

Rinderbraten
Roast beef

Rippchen mit Sauerkraut
Pickled ribs of pork with *sauerkraut*

Rollmops
Herring fillets marinated in a vinegary liquid and filled with small pieces of onion, gherkins and white peppercorns

Rösti
Fried, diced potatoes mixed with small fried bacon cubes (Switzerland)

Rühreí
Scrambled egg

Salatplatte
Selection of salads

Sauerbraten
Marinated roast beef

Sauerkraut
Shredded, white, salted and fermented cabbage

Schlachtplatte
A mixture of cold sausages and meats

Schweinebraten
Roast pork

Schweinekotelett
Pork chop dipped in egg and breadcrumbs and fried

Schweinskarrée
Pork cutlets cooked in one piece (Austria)

Schweizer Käse
see *Emmentaler* (Switzerland)

Semmelknödel
Whole roll dumpling (Austria)

Spätzle
Home-made noodles served with breadcrumbs and browned butter

Spiegelei
Fried egg

Strammer Max
Fried egg with raw ham and rye bread

Tilsiter
Savoury, straw-coloured cheese; slightly sour and sharpish taste with a smooth consistency

Tiroler Eierspeise
Hard boiled eggs, potatoes, cream, anchovies, topped with breadcrumbs and baked in the oven (Austria)

Topfen
Curd cheese (Austria)

Topfenknödel
Curd cheese dumplings sprinkled with fried bread-crumbs (Austria)

Urner Kraut mit Reis
Cooked cabbage strips mixed with cheese and cooked rice, with fried onion

Weckklöße
Bread dumplings

Eating & Drinking
Menu Reader

Wiener Schnitzel
Veal escalope fried in breadcrumbs

Wiener Fischfilets
Fish fillets baked with soured cream, gherkins and capers

Wildgulasch
Game stew

Wildbraten
Roast venison

Wildsuppe
Game soup

Zwiebelsuppe
Onion soup

Desserts

Apfelkompott
Stewed apple

Apfelmus
Apple sauce

Apfelrösti
Cooked apple slices fried in butter together with bread slices (Switzerland)

Auflauf
Soufflé

Eis(creme)
Ice Cream

Eisbecher
Rather like a Knickerbocker Glory

Kaiserschmarren
Pieces of chopped-up batter with raisins, sugar and cinnamon

Palatschinken
Pancakes filled with curd cheese mixture, or with apricot jam

Rote Grütze
Raspberry, red currant and wine jelly served with fresh cream

Salzburger Nockerl
Foamy omelette-cum-soufflé with a very light centre and a puffed and golden outside (Austria)

Weincreme
Wine creme

Zwetschkenknödel
Boiled plum dumplings fried in breadcrumbs, sprinkled with sugar, and served hot (Austria)

Eating & Drinking
The Wine List

When choosing German wines it helps to know some of the terms used to describe them. An ordinary wine is called a *Tafelwein.* Higher quality wines will be described as *Qualitätswein*, *Kabinett*, or, best of all, *mit Prädikat.* The words *Auslese* and *Beerenauslese* tell you that the wine is made from specially selected grapes. *Trockenbeerauslese* means that the grapes have been left to ripen well after the rest of the harvest so as to give rich, sweet dessert wines. *Spätlese* indicates a late gathered wine. An *Eiswein* is one of the rarest wines of all: the grapes are not gathered till mid-winter and give a wine with a honey-sweet, liqueur-like consistency.

Baden
A district famous for its white wine

Bernkasteler
A fine Moselle white wine

Burgenland
A part of Austria which produces some pleasant table wines

Burgunder
A full-bodied red wine

Gewürztraminer
A full-bodied white wine

Gutedel
A very dry white wine

Heuriger
The Austrian term for *Neuer Wein*

Johannisberg
A Swiss wine made from Sylvaner and Riesling grapes, usually medium dry

Kalterersee
A soft red wine from the southern Tyrol

Kreuznacher
A Nahe wine of fine quality

Liebfraumilch
One of the best known of all white Rheinhessen wines, medium dry to sweet

Müller-Thurgau
A very pleasant white wine

Neuer Wein/Heuriger (Austria)
The first new wine drunk just after the harvest when the grape juice just starts fermenting

Neuberger
One of the best Franconian wines

Niersteiner
A medium dry to sweet Rheinhessen wine

Oppenheimer
One of the best medium dry to sweet wines from Rheinhessen

Riesling
A medium dry white wine

Eating & Drinking
The Wine List

Rudesheimer
One of the best dry and full-bodied Rheingau wines

Ruländer
A heavy-bodied white wine

Schaumwein
A sparkling wine

Sekt
The German equivalent of French champagne

Spätburgunder Rotwein
An excellent full-bodied red wine

Sylvaner
A medium dry white wine

Veitshoechheimer
A good Franconian wine

Weißherbst/Schwarzriesling
A rosé

Eating & Drinking
What to Drink

Germans do not have separate places for eating and drinking: at a *Wirtshaus* you can have a good meal or a snack, but you can also just sit and have a drink at any time of day. You will be served at your table, and you pay for your drinks as you leave rather than when the waitress brings them to you. In country areas especially you may see a table with a sign *Stammtisch* on it; don't sit down there – it is a sort of 'club-table' reserved for the regulars. A particularly lively time to visit the *Wirtshaus* for a bit of local colour is Sunday morning, when people gather for a drink and a chat after church.

ein Achtel Weißwein — a glass of white wine
ine ***ahkh****-tèl* ***vice****-vine*

einen Cognac — a brandy
ine*-èn* ***kon****-yak*

ein Achtel Rotwein — a glass of red wine
ine ***ahkh****-tèl-****rot*** *vine*

eine Halbe — a large beer
ine*-è* ***hal****-bè*

You might like to try one of the many varieties of *Schnaps*:

einen Steinhäger — juniper brandy
ine*-èn* ***shtine****-hay-gèr*

einen Himbeergeist — raspberry brandy
ine*-èn* ***him****-bay-èr-gye-st*

ein Kirschwasser — kirsch
ine ***keersh****-vass-èr*

einen Kümmel — caraway liqueur
ine*-èn* ***koo̅****-mèl*

einen Dornkaat — strong juniper gin
ine*-èn* ***dorn****-kaht*

If you want a soft drink for yourself or the children:

eine Cola — coke
ine*-è* ***kō****-la*

einen Apfelsaft — apple juice
ine*-èn* ***ap****-fèl-zaft*

einen Traubensaft — grape juice
ine*-èn* ***trow****-bèn-zaft*

einen Orangensaft — orange juice
ine*-èn o-****ran****-jèn-zaft*

eine Limonade — fizzy drink
ine*-è lee-mō-****nah****-dè*

Eating & Drinking
Coffee & Cakes

Another German institution is the *Konditorei*, or *Kaffeehaus*, as it is known in Austria. This is the café and confectionery shop where you go for *Kaffee und Kuchen*, coffee and cakes, though you can also have something stronger if you prefer.

einen Kaffee coffee
ine-èn ka-fay

einen Kaffee mit Milch coffee with milk
ine-èn ka-fay mit milkh

einen Tee mit Milch tea with milk
ine-èn tay mit milkh

einen Tee mit Zitrone lemon tea
ine-èn tay mit tsi-trō-nè

You can simply point to one of the tempting cakes on display and say "*geben Sie mir bitte das da*", but it's worth knowing the names of a few of the best known:

Berliner Pfannkuchen – Doughnuts with jam
ber-lee-nèr pfan-koo-khèn

Gugelhupf – Ring-shaped yeast-cake with fruit
goo-gèl-hoopf

Käsekuchen – Cheesecake
kay-ze-koo-khèn

Linzertorte – Round cake with layers of almond-flavoured pastry and jam
lin-tser-tor-tè

Sachertorte – Chocolate sponge cake with chocolate icing and apricot filling
zakh-èr-tor-tè

Schwarzwälder Kirschtorte – Black Forest cherry gateau
shvarts-vel-dèr keersh-tor-tè

You can sometimes get savoury snacks, but there is not usually a great selection. You might find these:

belegtes Brot open sandwich
bè-layg-tès brōt

Ochsenschwanzsuppe oxtail soup
okh-sèn-shvants-zoo-pè

belegtes Brötchen filled roll
bè-layg-tès brur't-khèn

Königinpastete chicken vol-au-vent
kur'-nig-in-pass-tay-tè

Paying

These phrases are needed in all sorts of places besides shops, so they have been collected together here.

How much is that? – Wieviel kostet das?
*vee-**feel kos**-tèt dass?*

I can't afford that much – Das kann ich mir nicht leisten
*dass kan ikh meer nikht **lice**-tèn*

What does that come to? – Was macht das?
*vass **makht** dass?*

How much is it – **to get in?**
Wieviel kostet der Eintritt?
*vee **feel kos**-tèt der **ine**-trit?*

– **for a child?**
es für ein Kind?
es fōōr ine kint?

– **to phone to Britain?**
ein Anruf nach Großbritannien?
*ine **an**-roof nahkh grōss-bri-**tan**-yèn?*

How much is it – **per person?**
Wieviel kostet das pro Person?
*vee-**feel kos**-tèt dass prō per-**zōn**?*

– **per night?**
pro Nacht?
prō nakht?

– **per kilo?**
pro Kilo?
*prō **kee**-lō?*

– **per metre?**
pro Meter?
*prō **may**-ter?*

– **per kilometre?**
pro Kilometer?
*prō kee-lō-**may**-ter?*

Are service and tax included? – Sind Bedienung und Mehrwertsteuer inbegriffen?
*sint bè-**dee**-noong oont **mer**-vert-shtoy-èr **in**-bè-grif-èn?*

Paying

Is there any extra charge? –	Gibt es einen Preiszuschlag? *gipt es **ine**-èn **price**-tsoo-shlahg?*
Do I pay a deposit? –	Muß ich eine Anzahlung machen? *mooss ikh **ine**-è **an**-tsahl-oong **makh**-èn?*
Do I pay in advance or afterwards? –	Zahle ich im voraus oder später? ***tsahl**-è ikh im fo-**rows** **ō**-dèr **shpay**-tèr?*
Do you accept traveller's cheques? –	Nehmen Sie Reiseschecks? ***nay**-mèn zee **rye**-zè-sheks?*
I want to pay by credit card –	Ich möchte mit Kreditkarte bezahlen *ikh **mur'kh**-tè mit kre-**deet**-kar-tè bè-**tsahl**-èn*
Can I have an itemized bill? –	Kann ich eine ausführliche Rechnung haben? *kan ikh **ine**-è **ows**-fōōr-likh-è **rekh**-noong **hah**-bèn?*
Can I have a receipt? –	Kann ich eine Quittung haben? *kan ikh **ine**-è **kvi**-toong **hah**-bèn?*
I haven't enough money –	Ich habe nicht genug Geld bei mir *ikh **hah**-bè nikht gè-**nook** gelt bye meer*
You've given me the wrong change –	Sir haben mir falsch herausgegeben *zee **hah**-bèn meer falsh he-**rows**-gè-**gay**-bèn*
Please forward it to this address –	Bitte senden Sie es an diese Adresse nach ***bit**-è **zen**-dèn zee es an **dee**-zè a-**dress**-è nahkh*
Please pack it carefully –	Bitte verpacken Sie es sorgfältig ***bit**-è fer-**pak**-èn zee es **zorg**-fel-tikh*

The Basic Phrases

Whatever it is you want to buy, you'll need some of these phrases.

I would like Ich hätte gerne *ikh **het**-è **gern**-è*	– **a box of matches** eine Schachtel Streichhölzer ***ine**-è **shakh**-tèl **shtrye**-khur'l-tser*
	– **some stamps** ein paar Briefmarken *ine par **breef**-mar-kèn*
Do you sell sunglasses?	– Verkaufen Sie Sonnenbrillen? *fer-**kow**-fèn zee **zon**-èn-bril-èn?*
Have you got any Haben Sie ***hah**-bèn zee*	– **English newspapers?** englische Zeitungen? ***eng**-lish-è **tsye**-toong-èn?*
	– **toothpaste?** Zahnpasta? ***tsahn**-pas-ta?*
I need some suntan oil	– Ich brauche etwas Sonnenöl *ikh **brow**-khè **et**-vas **zon**-èn-ur'l*
Where is Wo ist *vō ist*	– **the shoe department?** die Schuhabteilung? *dee **shoo**-ap-tile-oong?*
	– **the food department?** die Lebensmittelabteilung? *dee **lay**-bènz-mi-tèl-**ap**-tile-oong?*
Can I see Kann ich *kan ikh*	– **the hat in the window?** den Hut im Schaufenster sehen? *dayn hoot im **show**-fen-ster **zay**-èn?*
	– **that hat over there?** den Hut dort sehen? ***dayn** hoot dort **zay**-èn?*
No, the other one	– Nein, den anderen ***nine**, dayn **an**-dè-rèn*
Have you got Haben Sie ***hah**-bèn zee*	– **a larger one?** einen größeren? – ***ine**-èn **grur'**-sèr-èn?*
	– **a smaller one?** einen kleineren? ***ine**-èn **kline**-èr-èn?*

The Basic Phrases

I'm just looking – Ich schaue mich nur etwas um
ikh ***show****-è mikh* ***noor et****-vas oom*

I'm looking for a blouse – Ich hätte gerne eine Bluse
ikh ***het****-è* ***gern****-è* ***ine****-è* ***bloo****-zè*

I like this one – Diese hier gefällt mir
dee*-zè heer gè-****felt*** *meer*

I don't like it – Sie gefällt mir nicht
*zee gè-****felt*** *meer nikht*

Have you got anything cheaper? – Haben Sie etwas Billigeres?
hah*-bèn zee* ***et****-vas* ***bil****-ig-èr-ès?*

I'll take Ich nehme *ikh* ***nay****-mè*
– **this one**
diese hier
dee*-zè heer*

– **that one**
jene dort
yay*-nè dort*

– **the other one**
die andere
dee ***an****-dè-rè*

Please wrap it up – Bitte verpacken Sie es
bit*-è fer-****pak****-èn zee es*

There's no need to wrap it, thank you – Danke, Sie brauchen es nicht zu verpacken
dang*-kè, zee* ***brow****-khèn es nikht tsoo ver-****pak****-èn*

Can I have a plastic bag? – Kann ich eine Plastiktüte haben?
kan ikh ***ine****-è* ***pla****-stik-tōō-tè* ***hah****-bèn?*

Is there a reduction for children? – Gibt es eine Kinderermäßigung?
geebt es ***ine****-è* ***kind****-èr-er-****me****-si-gung?*

Food

Of course, you can solve all your language problems by heading for the nearest supermarket, but you will miss the personal touch of the shopkeepers and the people in the market.

I'd like – **a kilo of apples (2lb 3oz)**
Ich hätte gerne ein Kilo Äpfel
*ikh **het**-è **gern**-è ine **kee**-lō **ep**-fèl*

– **a pound of tomatoes (1lb 1oz)**
ein Pfund Tomaten
*ine pfoont tō-**mah**-tèn*

– **half a pound of butter (250gm/9oz)**
ein halbes Pfund Butter
*ine **hal**-bès pfoont **boo**-tèr*

– **100gm of ground coffee**
hundert Gramm gemahlenen Kaffee
***hoon**-dert gram gè-**mahl**-en-èn **ka**-fay*

– **5 slices of ham**
fünf Scheiben Schinken
*fōōnf **shye**-bèn **shing**-kèn*

– **half a dozen eggs**
sechs Eier
*zekhs **eye**-èr*

A bag of sugar, please – Ein Paket Zucker, bitte
*ine pa-**kayt** **tsoo**-kèr **bit**-è*

A litre of milk, please – Einen Liter Milch, bitte
***ine**-èn **lee**-tèr milkh **bit**-è*

A bottle of wine, please – Eine Flasche Wein, bitte
***ine**-è **flash**-è vine, **bit**-è*

Two pork chops, please – Zwei Schweinekoteletts, bitte
*tsvye **shvine**-è-kot-è-**lets** **bit**-è*

A lamb joint, please – Eine Lammkeule, bitte
***ine**-è **lam**-koy-lè, **bit**-è*

A steak, please – Ein Steak, bitte
*ine shtayk, **bit**-è*

Food

Groceries

baby food	Babynahrung ***bay**-bee-nah-roong*	**milk**	Milch *milkh*
biscuits	Kekse ***kayk**-sè*	**mustard**	Senf *zenf*
bread	Brot *brōt*	**oil**	Öl *ur'l*
butter	Butter ***boo**-tèr*	**pepper**	Pfeffer ***pfe**-fèr*
cheese	Käse ***kay**-zè*	**rice**	Reis *rice*
coffee	Kaffee ***ka**-fay*	**salt**	Salz *zalts*
cream	Sahne ***zah**-nè*	**soup**	Suppe ***zoo**-pè*
eggs	Eier ***eye**-èr*	**sugar**	Zucker ***tsoo**-kèr*
flour	Mehl *mayl*	**tea**	Tee *tay*
jam	Marmelade *mar-mè-**lah**-dè*	**vinegar**	Essig *essikh*
margarine	Margarine *mar-ga-**ree**-nè*	**yoghurt**	Joghurt ***yō**-goort*

Meat

beef	Rindfleisch ***rint**-flye-sh*	**liver**	Leber ***lay**-bèr*
chicken	Huhn *hoon*	**kidneys**	Nieren ***nee**-rèn*
ham	Schinken ***shing**-kèn*	**pork**	Schweinefleisch ***shvye**-nè-flye-sh*
lamb	Lamm *lam*	**veal**	Kalbfleisch ***kalp**-flye-sh*

Fish

cod	Kabeljau ***kah**-bèl-yow*	**mussels**	Muscheln ***moosh**-èln*
hake	Stockfisch ***shtok**-fish*	**sole**	Seezunge ***zay**-tsoong-è*
herring	Hering ***hay**-ring*	**trout**	Forelle *for-**el**-è*

Food
Fruit & Vegetables

apples	Äpfel ***ep**-fèl*	**celery**	Stangensellerie ***shtan**-gèn-ze-lè-ree*
apricots	Aprikosen *a-pri-**kō**-zèn*	**cherries**	Kirschen ***keer**-shèn*
artichoke	Artischocke *ar-ti-**shōk**-è*	**chervil**	Kerbel ***ker**-bèl*
asparagus	Spargel ***shpar**-gèl*	**chicory**	Chicorée ***shi**-ko-ray*
aubergine	Aubergine ***ō**-ber-jee-nè*	**chives**	Schnittlauch ***shnit**-lowkh*
avocado	Avocado *a-vo-**kah**-dō*	**courgettes**	Zucchini *tsoo-**kee**-nee*
bananas	Bananen *ba-**nah**-nèn*	**cucumber**	Gurke ***goor**-kè*
basil	Basilienkraut *ba-**zi**-lee-yen-krowt*	**dates**	Datteln ***dat**-èln*
bayleaf	Lorbeerblatt ***lor**-bay-èr-blat*	**eggplant**	Aubergine ***ō**-ber-jee-nè*
beetroot	rote Rübe ***rōt**-è **rōō**-bè*	**French beans**	grüne Bohnen ***grōō**-nè **bō**-nèn*
blackcurrants	schwarze Johannisbeeren ***shvar**-tsè yō-**ha**-niss-bay-èr-èn*	**garlic**	Knoblauch ***knōp**-lowkh*
		gherkin	Gewürzgurke *gè-**vōōrts**-goor-kè*
broad beans	Saubohnen ***zow**-bōn-èn*	**grapefruit**	Grapefruit ***grayp**-froot*
Brussels sprouts	Rosenkohl ***rō**-zèn-kōl*	**grapes**	Trauben ***trow**-bèn*
cabbage	Kohl *kōl*	**greengages**	Reineclaude *ren-è-**klō**-dè*
carrots	Karotten *ka-**rot**-èn*	**green pepper**	grüner Paprika ***grōō**-ner **pa**-pri-ka*
cauliflower	Blumenkohl ***bloo**-mèn-kōl*	**leek**	Lauch *lowkh*
celeriac	Sellerie ***ze**-lè-ree*	**lemon**	Zitrone *tsi-**trō**-nè*

Food

Fruit & Vegetables

lettuce	Kopfsalat *__kopf__-zal-aht*	**radish**	Rettich *__re__-tikh*
marrow	Kürbis *__kōōr__-biss*	**raspberries**	Himbeeren *__him__-bay-èr-èn*
mint	Pfefferminze *__pfe__-fèr-mints-è*	**red pepper**	roter Paprika *__rō__-ter __pa__-pri-ka*
melon	Melone *me-__lō__-nè*	**rosemary**	Rosmarin *roz-ma-__reen__*
mushrooms	Pilze *__pil__-tsè*	**sage**	Salbei *zal-__bye__*
olives	Oliven *ō-__lee__-vèn*	**shallots**	Schalotten *sha-__lot__-èn*
onions	Zwiebeln *__tsvee__-bèln*	**spinach**	Spinat *shpi-__naht__*
oranges	Orangen *o-__ran__-jèn*	**squash**	Kürbis *__kōōr__-biss*
parsley	Petersilie *pay-tèr-__zee__-li-yè*	**strawberries**	Erdbeeren *__ert__-bay-èr-èn*
parsnip	Pastinake *pass-ti-__nah__-kè*	**sweetcorn**	Mais *mice*
peach	Pfirsich *__pfeer__-zikh*	**thyme**	Thymian *__tōō__-mi-yahn*
pears	Birnen *__beer__-nèn*	**tomatoes**	Tomaten *tō-__mah__-tèn*
peas	Erbsen *__erp__-sèn*	**tarragon**	Estragon *__es__-tra-gon*
pineapple	Ananas *__a__-na-nass*	**turnip**	Steckrübe *__shtek__-rōō-bè*
plums	Pflaumen *__pflow__-mèn*	**watercress**	Brunnenkresse *__broo__-nèn-kre-sè*
pomegranates	Granatäpfel *gra-__naht__-ep-fèl*	**watermelon**	Wassermelone *__vass__-er-me-lō-nè*
potatoes	Kartoffeln *kar-__tof__-èln*	**zucchini**	Zucchini *tsoo-__kee__-nee*
red radishes	Radieschen *ra-__dees__-khèn*		

Newspapers & Stationery

If you want a newspaper, you'll get it at a news stand, *Zeitungskiosk*, while stationery is generally sold in a *Schreibwarenhandlung*.

Have you got any – **English newspapers?**
Haben Sie englische Zeitungen?
***hah**-bèn zee* ***eng**-lish-è **tsye**-toong-èn?*

– **American newspapers?**
amerikanische Zeitungen?
*a-me-ri-**kahn**-ish-è **tsye**-toong-èn?*

– **postcards?**
Postkarten?
***post**-kar-tèn?*

I would like – **some notepaper**
Ich hätte gerne etwas Schreibpapier
*ikh **het**-è **gern**-è* ***et**-vas **shripe**-pa-peer*

– **some envelopes**
ein paar Briefumschläge
*ine par **breef**-oom-shlay-gè*

– **a pen**
einen Füller
***ine**-èn **fōō**-ler*

– **a pencil**
einen Bleistift
***ine**-èn **blye**-shtift*

I need – **a bottle of ink**
Ich brauche ein Glas Tinte
*ikh **brow**-khè* *ine glass **tin**-tè*

– **some adhesive tape**
Klebstreifen
***kleb**-shtrye-fèn*

Do you sell – **English paperbacks?**
Führen Sie englische Taschenbücher?
***fōō**-rèn zee* ***eng**-lish-è **tash**-èn-bōō-kher?*

– **street maps?**
Stadtpläne?
***shtat**-play-nè?*

Cigarettes

A packet of . . . please –	Eine Schachtel . . . bitte ***ine**-è **shakh**-tèl . . . **bit**-è*
with filter-tip –	mit Filter *mit **fil**-ter*
without filter –	ohne Filter *ō-nè **fil**-ter*
Have you got any American brands? –	Führen Sie amerikanische Zigaretten? ***foo**-rèn zee a-me-ri-**kahn**-ish-è tsi-ga-**re**-tèn?*
Have you got any English brands? –	Führen Sie englische Zigaretten? ***foo**-rèn zee **eng**-lish-è tsi-ga-**re**-tèn?*
A pipe –	Eine pfeiffe ***ine**-è **pfye**-fè*
A pouch of pipe tobacco –	Ein Päckchen Pfeifentabak *ine **pek**-khèn **pfye**-fèn-ta-bak*
Some pipe cleaners –	Ein Päckchen Pfeifenreiniger *ine **pek**-khèn **pfye**-fèn-**rye**-ni-gèr*
A box of matches –	Eine Schachtel Streichhölzer ***ine**-è **shakh**-tèl **shtrye**-khur'l-tsèr*
A cigar –	Eine Zigarre ***ine**-è tsi-**ga**-rè*
A cigarette lighter –	Ein Feuerzeug *ine **foy**-er-tsoyk*
A gas (butane) refill –	Eine Gaspatrone ***ine**-è **gahs**-pa-**trō**-nè*

The Chemist/Druggist

You should see the *If you're Ill* section if anybody is really unwell, but a chemist(*Apotheke*), should be able to help you with minor ailments. There will be an illuminated sign outside, a red *A* on a white background. He won't sell the range of toiletries stocked by chemists at home – for some of the items on the next page you will have to go to a *Drogerie*.

I want something for –	**a headache**
Ich hätte gerne etwas gegen	Kopfschmerzen
*ikh **het**-è **gern**-è **et**-vas **gay**-gèn*	***kopf**-shmer-tsèn*
–	**insect bites**
	Insektenstiche
	*in-**zek**-tèn-shtikh-è*
How many do I take? –	Wieviele soll ich nehmen?
	*vee-**feel**-è zol ikh **nay**-mèn?*
How often do I take them? –	Wie oft muß ich sie nehmen?
	*vee **oft** mooss ikh zee **nay**-mèn?*
Are they safe for children to take? –	Sind sie für Kinder geeignet?
	*zint zee fo͞or **kin**-der gè-**ige**-nèt?*

You might also want something for:

chapped skin	rissige Haut ***riss**-i-gè howt*	**sunburn**	Sonnenbrand ***zon**-èn-brant*
a cold	Erkältung *er-**kel**-toong*	**swollen feet**	geschwollene Füße *gè-**shvol**-en-è **fo͞o**-sè*
a cough	Husten ***hoo**-stèn*	**toothache**	Zahnschmerzen ***tsahn**-shmer-tsèn*
hay fever	Heuschnupfen ***hoy**-shnoop-fèn*	**an upset stomach**	Magenschmerzen ***mah**-gèn-shmer-tsèn*
a sore throat	Halsschmerzen ***hals**-shmer-tsèn*		

or need some of the items on the next page.

The Chemist/Druggist

English	German	Pronunciation
aftershave	Aftershave	***af***-*tèr-shavv*
anti-histamine	Antihistamin	*an-ti-his-ta-**meen***
antiseptic	Antiseptikum	*an-ti-**zep**-ti-koom*
aspirin	Aspirin	*as-pi-**reen***
bandage	Verband	*fer-**bant***
band-aid	Heftpflaster	***heft***-*pfla-stèr*
bath salts	Badesalz	***bah***-*dè-zalts*
bubble bath	Schaumbad	***showm***-*baht*
cleansing milk	Reinigungsmilch	***rye***-*ni-goongz-milkh*
contraceptive	Verhütungsmittel	*fer-**hōō**-toongz-mi-tèl*
cotton wool	Watte	***va***-*tè*
deodorant	Deodorant	*day-ō-do-**rant***
disinfectant	Desinfektionsmittel	*dayz-in-fek-tsi-**yōnz**-mi-tèl*
eau de Cologne	Eau de Cologne	*ō-dè-ko-**lon**-yè*
eye shadow	Lidschatten	***leet***-*sha-tèn*
hair spray	Haarspray	***har***-*shpray*
hand cream	Handcreme	***hant***-*kraym*
insect repellant	Insektenschutz-mittel	*in-**zek**-tèn-shoots-mi-tèl*
Kleenex	Kleenex	***klee***-*nex*
laxative	Abführmittel	***ap***-*fōōr-mi-tèl*
lipstick	Lippenstift	***li***-*pèn-shtift*
mascara	Wimperntusche	***vim***-*pern-too-shè*
mouthwash	Mundwasser	***moont***-*vass-er*
nail file	Nagelfeile	***nah***-*gèl-fye-lè*
nail varnish	Nagellack	***nah***-*gèl-lak*
nail varnish remover	Nagellackentferner	***nah***-*gèl-lak-ent-**fer**-nèr*
perfume	Parfüm	*par-**fōōm***
powder	Puder	***poo***-*der*
razor blades	Rasierklingen	*ra-**zeer**-kling-èn*
sanitary towels (napkins)	Damenbinden	***dah***-*mèn-bin-dèn*
shampoo	Shampoo	***sham***-*poo*
shaving cream	Rasiercreme	*ra-**zeer**-kraym*
skin mois-turizer	Feuchtigkeits-creme	***foykh***-*tikh-kites-kraym*
soap	Seife	***zife***-*è*
suntan oil	Sonnenöl	***zon***-*èn-ur'l*
talc	Körperpuder	***kur'***-*pèr-poo-dèr*
toilet water	Toilettenwasser	*tō-a-**le**-tèn-vass-er*
toothpaste	Zahnpasta	***tsahn***-*pas-ta*

Camera Shop

I need a film – **for this camera**
Ich brauche einen Film für diese Kamera
ikh ***brow****-khè* ***ine****-èn film* *fōōr* ***dee****-zè* ***kam****-è-ra*

– **for this cine camera**
für diese Filmkamera
fōōr ***dee****-zè* ***film****-kam-è-ra*

I want – **a black and white film**
Ich hätte gerne einen Schwarzweißfilm
ikh ***he****-tè* ***gern****-è* ***ine****-èn* ***shvarts****-vice-film*

– **a colour print film**
einen Farbfilm
ine*-èn* ***farp****-film*

– **a colour slide film**
einen Diafarbfilm
ine*-èn* ***dee****-a-farp-film*

– **batteries for the flash**
Batterien für das Blitzgerät
*ba-tè-****ree****-yèn fōōr dass* ***blits****-gè-rayt*

Can you develop this film, please? – Würden Sie bitte diesen Film entwickeln?
vōōr*-dèn zee* ***bit****-è* ***dee****-zèn film ent-****vik****-èln?*

I would like two prints of this one – Ich hätte gerne zwei Abzüge davon
ikh ***he****-tè* ***gern****-è tsvye* ***ap****-zōō-gè da-****fon***

When will the photos be ready? – Wann werden die Bilder fertig sein?
van ***ver****-dèn dee* ***bil****-dèr* ***fer****-tikh zine?*

I would like this photo enlarged – Ich hätte gerne eine Vergrößerung von diesem Bild
ikh ***he****-tè* ***gern****-è* ***ine****-è fer-****grur'****-sè-roong fon* ***dee****-zèm bilt*

There is something wrong with my camera – Mit meiner Kamera stimmt etwas nicht
mit ***mine****-er* ***kam****-è-ra shtimt* ***et****-vas nikht*

The film is jammed – Der Film klemmt
der film klemt

Camera Shop
Cameras & Accessories

accessory Zubehör *__tsoo__-bè hur'r*
blue filter Blaufilter *__blow__-fil-ter*
cassette Kassettenfilm *ka-__set__-èn-film*
cartridge Filmpatrone *__film__-pa-__trō__-nè*
cine camera Filmkamera *__film__-kam-è-ra*
distance Entfernung *ent-__fer__-noong*
enlargement Vergrößerung *fer-__grur'__-sè-roong*
exposure Belichtung *bè-__likh__-toong*
exposure meter Belichtungsmesser *bè-__likh__-toongz-mess-èr*
flash Blitzlicht *__blits__-likht*
flash bulb Blitzlichtlampe *__blits__-likht-lam-pè*
flash cube Blitzwürfel *__blits__-vōōr-fèl*
focal distance Brennweite *__bren__-vye-tè*
focus Brennpunkt *__bren__-poonkt*
in focus scharf *sharf*
out of focus unscharf *__un__-sharf*
image Bild *bilt*
lens Linse *__lin__-zè*
lens cover Objektivschutzkappe *ob-yek-__teef__-shoots-ka-pè*
over exposed überbelichtet *__ōō__-ber-bè-likh-tèt*
picture Aufnahme *__owf__-nah-mè*
projector Projektor *pro-__yek__-tor*
print Abzug *__ap__-tsook*
negative Negativ *nay-ga-__teef__*
red filter Rotfilter *__rōt__-fil-ter*
reel Filmspule *__film__-shpoo-lè*
rewind mechanism Rückspulmechanismus *__rōōk__-shpool-mekh-a-__nis__-moos*
shade Blende *__blen__-dè*
slide Diapositiv *dee-ya-pō-zi-__teef__*
shutter Verschluß *fer-__shlooss__*
shutter speed Verschlußgeschwindigkeit *fer-__shlooss__-gè-shvin-dikh-kite*
transparency Lichtbild *__likht__-bilt*
tripod Stativ *shta-__teef__*
under exposed unterbelichtet *__oon__-ter-bè-likh-tèt*
viewfinder Sucher *__zookh__-èr*
wide-angle lens Weitwinkelobjektiv *__vite__-ving-kèl-ob-yek-__teef__*
yellow filter Gelbfilter *__gelp__-fil-ter*

Clothes Sizes

First of all, you'll want some idea of your continental size. Unfortunately, slight variations in sizes mean that these can only be approximate equivalents.

Dresses

UK	10	12	14	16
US	8	10	12	14
Germany	36	38	40	42

Ladies' sweaters

UK/US	32	34	36	38	40
Germany	42	44	46	48	50

Ladies shoes

UK	4½	5	5½	6	6½	7
US	6	6½	7	7½	8	8½
Germany	37½	38	38½	39	40	40½

Men's shoes

UK	8	9	10	11
US	9½	10½	11½	12½
Germany	42	43	44	45½

Clothes Sizes

Men's suits

UK/US	36	38	40	42	44	46
Germany	46	48	50	52	54	56

Waist and chest measurements

inches	28	30	32	34	36	38	40
centimetres	71	76	81	87	91	97	102
inches	42	44	46	48	50	52	54
centimetres	107	112	117	122	127	132	138

Men's shirts

UK/US	14	14½	15	15½	16	16½	17
Germany	36	37	38	39	41	42	43

Clothes

I would like – **a dress**
Ich hätte gerne – ein Kleid
*ikh **he**-tè **gern**-è* – *ine klite*

– **a sweater**
einen Pullover
***ine**-èn poo-**lō**-vèr*

I take a continental size 40 – Ich habe Größe vierzig
*ikh **hah**-bè **grur'**-sè **feer**-tsikh*

I take a shoe size 40 – Ich habe Schuhgröße vierzig
*ikh **hah**-bè **shoo**-grur'-sè **feer**-tsikh*

Can you measure me? – Können Sie an mir Maß nehmen?
***kur'n**-èn zee an meer mahs **nay**-mèn?*

Have you got this in blue? – Haben Sie das gleiche in blau?
***hah**-bèn zee dass **glye**-khè in blow?*

What is the material? – Was ist das für ein Material?
*vass ist dass fōōr ine ma-tay-ri-**yahl**?*

I like – **this one**
Ich mag – dieses
ikh mahg – ***dee**-zès*

– **that one there**
das dort
***dass** dort*

– **the one in the window**
das im Schaufenster
***dass** im **show**-fen-stèr*

May I take it over to the light? – Kann ich es mal ans Licht halten?
*kan ikh es mal ans likht **hal**-tèn?*

May I try it on? – Kann ich es anprobieren?
*kan ikh es **an**-pro-bee-rèn?*

Where are the changing (dressing) rooms? – Wo sind die Umkleidekabinen?
*vō zint dee **oom**-klye-dè-ka-**bee**-nèn?*

I want a mirror – Ich hätte gerne einen Spiegel
*ikh **he**-tè **gern**-è **ine**-èn **shpee**-gèl*

I like it – Es gefällt mir
*es gè-**felt** meer*

Clothes

I don't like it – Es gefällt mir nicht
*es gè-**felt** meer nikht*

It doesn't fit – Es paßt nicht
*es **past** nikht*

It doesn't suit me – Es steht mir nicht
*es **shtayt** meer nikht*

I'd like one – **with a zip**
Ich hätte es gerne – mit einem Reißverschluß
*ikh **he**-tè es **gern**-è* – *mit **ine**-èm **rice**-fer-shlooss*

– **without a belt**
ohne Gürtel
*ō-nè **gōōr**-tèl*

Is this all you have? – Haben Sie sonst noch etwas?
***hah**-bèn zee **zonst** nokh **et**-vas?*

I'll take it – Ich nehme es
*ikh **nay**-mè es*

Is it washable? – Ist es waschbar?
*ist es **vash**-bar?*

Will it shrink? – Läuft es ein?
loyft es ine?

Must it be dry-cleaned? – Muß es chemisch gereinigt werden?
*mooss es **khay**-mish gè-**rye**-nikht **ver**-dèn?*

Clothes

blouse	Bluse ***bloo***-*zè*	**shorts**	Shorts *shorts*
bra	Büstenhalter ***bōō***-*sten-hal-tèr*	**skirt**	Rock *rok*
cardigan	Strickjacke ***shtrik***-*ya-kè*	**slip**	Unterrock ***oon***-*ter-rok*
coat	Mantel ***man***-*tèl*	**sneakers**	Segeltuchschuhe ***zay***-*gèl-tookh-* ***shoo***-*è*
dress	Kleid *klite*	**socks**	Socken ***zo***-*kèn*
dungarees	Latzhose ***lats***-*hō-zè*	**stockings**	Strümpfe ***shtrōōm***-*pfè*
gloves	Handschuhe ***hant***-*shoo-è*	**suit (man's)**	Anzug ***an***-*tsook*
hat	Hut *hoot*	**suit (woman's)**	Kostüm *kos-* ***tōōm***
jacket	Jacke ***ya***-*kè*	**sweater**	Pullover *poo-* ***lō***-*vèr*
jeans	Jeans *jeenz*	**swimming trunks**	Badehose ***bah***-*dè-hō-zè*
nightdress	Nachthemd ***nakht***-*hemt*	**swimsuit**	Badeanzug ***bah***-*dè-an-tsook*
panties	Schlüpfer ***shlōōp***-*fèr*	**tie**	Krawatte *kra-* ***va***-*tè*
petticoat	Petticoat ***pe***-*ti-cōt*	**tights**	Strumpfhose ***shtroompf***-*hō-zè*
pullover	Pullover *poo-* ***lō***-*vèr*	**towel**	Handtuch ***hant***-*tookh*
pyjamas	Pyjama *pōō-* ***jah***-*ma*	**trousers**	Hose ***hō***-*zè*
raincoat	Regenmantel ***ray***-*gèn-man-tèl*	**T shirt**	T-Shirt ***tee***-*shirt*
sandals	Sandalen *zan-* ***dah***-*lèn*	**underpants**	Unterhose ***oon***-*ter-hō-zè*
scarf	Schal *shahl*	**vest**	Unterhemd ***oon***-*ter-hemt*
shirt	Hemd *hemt*		

Clothes

Materials

acrylic Acryl *a-**kroōl***

corduroy Cord *kort*

cotton Baumwolle ***bowm**-vo-lè*

denim Denim *dè-**neem***

easy-care fabric pflegeleichtes Material ***pflayg**-è-lye-khtès ma-tay-ri-**yahl***

fur Pelz *pelts*

jersey Jersey ***jer**-zee*

lace Spitze ***shpi**-tsè*

leather Leder ***lay**-dèr*

linen Leinen ***line**-èn*

nylon Nylon ***nye**-lon*

polyester Polyester ***po**-loō-es-tèr*

poplin Popeline *po-pè-**leen***

rayon Rayon ***re**-yon*

silk Seide ***zye**-dè*

suede Wildleder ***vilt**-lay-dèr*

terylene Terylene *te-ree-**layn***

velvet Samt *zamt*

wool Wolle ***vo**-lè*

Accessories

bracelet Armband ***arm**-bant*

belt Gürtel ***goōr**-tèl*

brooch Brosche ***bro**-shè*

button Knopf *knopf*

earrings Ohrringe ***or**-ring-è*

handbag Handtasche ***hant**-tash-è*

handkerchief Taschentuch ***tash**-èn-tookh*

necklace Halskette ***hals**-ke-tè*

pendant Anhänger ***an**-heng-èr*

purse (UK) Geldbeutel ***gelt**-boy-tèl*

purse (US) Handtasche ***hant**-tash-è*

ring Ring *ring*

umbrella Regenschirm ***ray**-gèn-sheerm*

wallet Brieftasche ***breef**-tash-è*

watch Armbanduhr ***arm**-bant-**oo**-èr*

zip Reißverschluß ***rice**-fer-shlooss*

Hairdressers

I'd like to make an appointment – Ich möchte gerne einen Termin haben
*ikh **mur'kh**-tè **gern**-è **ine**-èn ter-**meen** **hah**-bèn*

I want – **a cut**
Ich möchte mein Haar geschnitten haben
*ikh **mur'kh**-tè mine har gè-**shni**-tèn **hah**-bèn*

– **a trim**
nachgeschnitten haben
*__nahkh__-gè-shni-tèn **hah**-bèn*

I want my hair – **fairly short**
Ich hätte mein Haar gerne ziemlich kurz geschnitten
*ikh **he**-tè mine har **gern**-è **tseem**-likh koorts gè-**shni**-tèn*

– **not too short**
nicht zu kurz geschnitten
*nikht tsoo koorts gè-**shni**-tèn*

– **short and curly**
kurz und lockig
*koorts oont **lo**-kikh*

– **layered**
stufig geschnitten
*__shtoo__-fikh gè-**shni**-tèn*

– **in a fringe**
mit Pony
*mit **po**-ni*

Take more off – **the front**
Bitte vorne kürzer
*__bit__-è **for**-nè **kōōr**-tsèr*

– **the back**
hinten kürzer
*__hin__-tèn **kōōr**-tsèr*

Not too much off – **the sides**
Bitte nicht zu kurz an den Seiten
*__bit__-è nikht tsoo koorts an dayn **zye**-tèn*

– **the top**
oben nicht zu kurz
ō-bèn nikht tsoo koorts

Hairdressers

I'd like – **a perm (permanent)**
Ich hätte gerne eine Dauerwelle
*ikh **he**-tè **gern**-è ine-è **dow**-èr-ve-lè*

– **a curly perm**
eine krause Dauerwelle
*ine-è **krow**-zè **dow**-èr-ve-lè*

– **a shampoo and set**
Waschen und Legen
*vash-èn oont **lay**-gèn*

– **a blow-dry**
mein Haar gesönnt
*mine har gè-**sur'nt***

– **my hair tinted**
eine Tönung
*ine-è **tur'**-noong*

– **my hair streaked**
eine Strähnenfärbung
*ine-è **shtray**-nèn-fer-boong*

The water is too hot – Das Wasser ist zu heiß
*dass **vass**-er ist tsoo hice*

The dryer is too hot – Die Trockenhaube ist zu heiß
*dee **tro**-kèn-how-bè ist tsoo hice*

I'd like – **a conditioner**
Ich hätte gerne eine Haarkur
*ikh **he**-tè **gern**-è ine-è **har**-koor*

– **hair spray**
etwas Haarspray
*et-vas **har**-shpray*

That's fine, thank you – Das ist schön so. Vielen Dank!
*dass ist shur'n zō. **fee**-lèn dank*

Dry Cleaners & Laundry

A dry cleaner's is called *eine Reinigung*; sometimes it is combined with a *Wäscherei* or laundry which will usually provide a fairly quick service. If you don't mind the chore of doing it yourself, you should look for *ein Waschsalon*.

Is there a launderette nearby? – Gibt es hier in der Nähe einen Waschsalon?
*gipt es heer in der **nay**-è **ine**-en **vash**-za-lon?*

Will you – **clean this skirt?**
Würden Sie bitte diesen Rock reinigen?
***vōōr**-dèn zee **bit**-è **dee**-zèn rok **rye**-ni-gèn?*

– **wash and iron these shirts?**
diese Hemden waschen und bügeln?
***dee**-zè **hem**-dèn **vash**-èn oont **bōō**-gèln?*

– **wash these clothes?**
diese Sachen waschen?
***dee**-zè **zakh**-èn **vash**-èn?*

This stain is – **grease**
Es ist ein Fettfleck
*es ist ine **fet**-flek*

– **ink**
Tintenfleck
***tin**-tèn-flek*

– **blood**
Blutfleck
***bloot**-flek*

– **coffee**
Kaffeefleck
***ka**-fay-flek*

This fabric is delicate – Der Stoff ist sehr empfindlich
*der shtof ist zer emp-**fint**-likh*

When will my things be ready? – Wann werden meine Sachen fertig sein?
*van **ver**-dèn **mine**-è **zakh**-èn **fer**-tikh zine?*

I need them in a hurry – Ich brauche sie sehr bald
*ikh **brow**-khè zee zer balt*

Repairs

I'm having trouble with my camera – Mit meiner Kamera ist etwas nicht in Ordnung
*mit **mine**-er **ka**-mè-ra ist **et**-vas nikht in **ord**-noong*

This is – **broken**
Das ist kaputt
*dass ist ka-**poot***

– **damaged**
beschädigt
*bè-**shay**-dikht*

– **torn**
zerrissen
*tser-**riss**-èn*

Would you have a look at this please? – Würden Sie sich das bitte anschauen?
***vōōr**-dèn zee zikh dass **bit**-è **an**-show-èn?*

Can you fix it? – Können Sie es reparieren?
***kur'n**-èn zee es re-pa-**ree**-rèn?*

Can you reheel these shoes? – Können Sie die Absätze erneuern?
***kur'n**-èn zee dee **ap**-ze-tsè er-**noy**-ern?*

Have you got a replacement part? – Haben Sie ein Ersatzteil?
***hah**-bèn zee ine er-**zats**-tile?*

When will it be ready? – Wann wird es fertig sein?
*van veert es **fer**-tikh zine?*

Can you do it quickly? – Können Sie es schnell erledigen?
***kur'n**-èn zee es shnel er-**lay**-di-gèn?*

Can you give me – **some strong glue?**
Können Sie mir bitte etwas starken Klebstoff geben?
***kur'n**-èn zee meer **bit**-è **et**-vas **shtar**-kèn **klayp**-shtof **gay**-bèn?*

– **some string?**
etwas Schnur geben?
***et**-vas shnoor **gay**-bèn?*

– **a needle and thread?**
Nadel und Faden
***nah**-dèl oont **fah**-dèn*

The Bank

Banks are usually open from 8 a.m. until 5 p.m. and most close for lunch. You can also change money at hotels, and, of course, *Wechselbüros*, but the rate of exchange tends to be less favourable.

Can I change – **these traveller's cheques?**
Kann ich hier diese Reiseschecks einlösen?
kan ikh heer ***dee**-zè **rye**-zè-sheks **ine**-lur'-zèn?*

– **these notes (bills)?**
Geld umtauschen?
***gelt oom**-tow-shèn?*

What is the rate for – **sterling?**
Was ist der Kurs für Pfund Sterling?
*vass ist der koors foor pfoont **ster**-ling?*

– **dollars?**
Dollars?
***do**-larz?*

Here is my passport – Hier ist mein Reisepaß
*heer ist mine **rye**-zè-pass*

I would like to cash a cheque with my Eurocheque card – Ich möchte gerne einen Euroscheck einlösen
*ikh **mur'kh**-tè **gern**-è **ine**-èn **oy**-rō-shek **ine**-lur'-zèn*

I would like to obtain a cash advance with my credit card – Ich möchte gerne Bargeld auf meine Kreditkarte haben
*ikh **mur'kh**-tè **gern**-è **bar**-gelt owf **mine**-è kre-**deet**-kar-tè **hah**-bèn*

What is your commission? – Wie hoch ist die Bearbeitungsgebühr?
*vee hōkh ist dee bè-**ar**-bye-toongz-gè-**boor**?*

Can you contact my bank to arrange for a transfer? – Könnten Sie mit meiner Bank eine Überweisung vereinbaren?
***kur'n**-tèn zee mit **mine**-er bank **ine**-è **oo**-ber-vye-zoong fer-**ine**-bah-rèn?*

This is the name and address of my bank – Hier sind Name and Adresse meiner Bank
*heer zint **nah**-mè oont a-**dress**-è **mine**-er bank*

Post Office

A German post office can be rather confusing with a long row of desks, each providing a specific service. The ones you are most likely to need are those dealing with stamps – *Briefmarken* – and parcels – *Pakete*.

How much is a letter – **to Britain?**
Wieviel kostet ein Brief nach Großbritannien?
***vee**-feel **kos**-tèt ine breef nahkh grōss-bri-**tan**-yèn?*

– **to the United States?**
in die Vereinigten Staaten?
*in dee fer-**ine**-ikh-tèn **shtah**-tèn?*

Six eighty Pfennig stamps, please – Sechs Briefmarken zu achtzig Pfennig, bitte
*zekhs **breef**-mark-èn tsoo **akh**-tsikh **pfe**-nikh, **bit**-è*

Can I have six stamps for postcards – **to Britain?**
Kann ich sechs Briefmarken haben für Postkarten nach Großbritannien?
*kan ikh zekhs **breef**-mark-èn **hah**-bèn fōōr **post**-kar-tèn nahkh grōss-bri-**tan**-yèn?*

– **to the United States?**
in die Vereinigten Staaten?
*in dee fer-**ine**-ikh-tèn **shtah**-tèn?*

I want to send this parcel – Ich möchte dieses Paket aufgeben
*ikh **mur'kh**-tè **dee**-zès pa-**kayt** **owf**-gay-bèn*

I want to send a telegram – Ich möchte ein Telegramm schicken
*ikh **mur'kh**-tè ine tay-lay-**gram** **shi**-kèn*

Can I have a telegram form, please? – Kann ich bitte ein Telegrammformular haben?
*kan ikh **bit**-è ine tay-lay-**gram**-for-moo-**lar** **hah**-bèn?*

When will it arrive? – Wann wird es ankommen?
*van veert es **an**-ko-mèn?*

I want to send this by registered mail – Ich möchte dies per Einschreiben schicken
*ikh **mur'kh**-tè dees per **ine**-shrye-bèn **shi**-kèn*

Using the Telephone

The simplest, but most expensive, way to telephone is from your hotel. Otherwise you can go to a post office – tell the clerk the number you want and she will direct you to a box. In some cases, as when phoning outside Germany, she will dial the call herself and charge you afterwards. In some cafés and restaurants you pay after you have made the call. The latest type of street telephones are in stainless steel and glass boxes; a green sign means you can make an international call. You will find numbers set out on page 110 and the telephone alphabet on page 114.

I would like to make a phone call to Britain	Ich möchte gerne nach Großbritannien anrufen *ikh* ***mur'kh****-tè* ***gern****-è nahkh grōss-bri-****tan****-yèn* ***an****-roo-fèn*
The number I want is . . . –	Die Nummer ist . . . *dee* ***noo****-mèr ist . . .*
I wish to make a reversed charge (collect) call –	Ich hätte gerne ein R-Gespräch *ikh* ***he****-tè* ***gern****-è ine* ***er****-gè-shpraykh*
Which box do I use? –	In welche Telefonzelle soll ich gehen? *in* ***velkh****-è tay-lay-****fōn****-tse-lè zol ikh* ***gay****-èn?*
May I use the telephone please? –	Kann ich bitte telefonieren? *kan ikh* ***bit****-è tay-lay-fō-****nee****-rèn?*
Please tell Mr. Braun to call me back –	Sagen Sie bitte Herrn Braun, er soll mich zurückrufen ***zah****-gèn zee* ***bit****-è* ***her****-èn brown er zol mikh zoo-****rōōk****-roo-fèn*
Can I speak to Mr. Braun? –	Kann ich bitte mit Herrn Braun sprechen? *kan ikh* ***bit****-è mit* ***her****-èn brown* ***shprekh****-èn?*
I have a crossed line –	Da ist jemand in der Leitung *dah ist* ***yay****-mant in der* ***lye****-toong*
We have been cut off –	Wir sind unterbrochen worden *veer zint oon-ter-****brokh****-èn* ***vor****-dèn*

Using the Telephone

You may hear somebody at the other end of the line telling you:

Braun – Hello, Mr. Braun speaking
brown

Ich verbinde Sie mit Herrn Braun – I'm putting you through to Mr. Braun
*ikh fer-**bin**-dè zee mit **her**-èn brown*

Moment, ich verbinde – I am trying to connect you
*mō-**ment**, ikh fer-**bin**-dè*

Es ist besetzt – The line is engaged (busy)
*es ist bè-**zetst***

Kein Anschluß unter dieser Nummer – This number is out of order
*kine **an**-shlooss **oon**-ter **dee**-zer **noo**-mèr*

Ich kann diese Nummer nicht erreichen – I cannot obtain this number
*ikh kan **dee**-zè **noo**-mèr nikht er-**rye**-khèn*

Bitte sprechen Sie – Please go ahead
***bit**-è **shprekh**-èn zee*

The Doctor
Accidents

If a visit to a doctor is necessary, you will probably have to pay on the spot. For visitors from Britain and Ireland, some of the cost of medical treatment is repayable under reciprocal EEC agreements (form E111 should be obtained before departure), but proper accident and medical insurance is still advisable. Ambulances also have to be paid for. You will find the number to call at the beginning of the phone book.

There has been an accident – Es ist ein Unfall passiert
*es ist ine **un**-fal pass-**eert***

Call an ambulance – Rufen Sie einen Krankenwagen
***roo**-fèn zee **ine**-èn **krang**-kèn-vah-gèn*

Get a doctor – Holen Sie einen Arzt
***hō**-lèn zee **ine**-èn artst*

He is unconscious – Er ist bewußtlos
*er ist bè-**voosst**-lōs*

He has been badly injured – Er ist schwer verletzt
*er ist shver fer-**letst***

Can I have an appointment with the doctor? – Kann ich einen Termin beim Arzt haben?
*kan ikh **ine**-èn ter-**meen** bime artst **hah**-bèn?*

I have cut myself – Ich habe mich geschnitten
*ikh **hah**-bè mikh gè-**shni**-tèn*

He has burnt himself – Er hat sich verbrannt
*er hat zikh fer-**brant***

She has a temperature – Sie hat Fieber
*zee hat **fee**-bèr*

I have hurt – **my arm**
Ich habe mir den Arm verletzt
*ikh **hah**-bè meer dayn arm fer-**letst***

– **my leg**
das Bein verletzt
*dass bine fer-**letst***

The Doctor
Accidents

I have had a fall – Ich bin hingefallen
*ikh bin **hin**-gè-fal-èn*

I have been stung – Ich bin gestochen worden
*ikh bin gè-**shtokh**-èn **vor**-dèn*

She has been bitten – Sie ist gebissen worden
*zee ist gè-**biss**-èn **vor**-dèn*

I have broken my arm – Ich habe mir den Arm gebrochen
*ikh **hah**-bè meer dayn **arm** gè-**brokh**-èn*

He has dislocated his shoulder – Er hat sich die Schulter verrenkt
*er hat zikh dee **shool**-tèr fer-**renkt***

She has sprained her ankle – Sie hat sich den Knöchel verstaucht
*zee hat zikh dayn **knur'kh**-èl fer-**shtowkht***

I have pulled a muscle – Ich habe eine Muskelzerrung
*ikh **hah**-bè **ine**-è **moos**-kèl-tse-roong*

There is a swelling here – Hier ist es geschwollen
*heer ist es gè-**shvol**-èn*

It is inflamed here – Hier ist es entzündet
*heer ist es ent-**tsōōn**-dèt*

I have a rash here – Ich habe hier einen Ausschlag
*ikh **hah**-bè heer **ine**-èn **ows**-shlahg*

I have a pain here – Ich habe hier Schmerzen
*ikh **hah**-bè heer **shmerts**-èn*

It is painful – **to walk**
Es tut weh — beim Laufen
es toot vay — *bime **low**-fèn*

– **to swallow**
beim Schlucken
*bime **shloo**-kèn*

– **to breathe**
beim Atmen
*bime **aht**-mèn*

I cannot sleep – Ich kann nicht schlafen
*ikh kan nikht **shlah**-fèn*

The Doctor
Symptoms

I have – **a headache**
Ich habe Kopfschmerzen
*ikh **hah**-bè **kopf**-shmerts-èn*

– **an earache**
Ohrenweh
***or**-èn-vay*

– **a sore throat**
Halsschmerzen
***hals**-shmer-tsèn*

– **cramp**
Krämpfe
***kraym**-pfè*

I have sunstroke – Ich habe einen Sonnenstich
*ikh **hah**-bè **ine**-èn **zo**-nèn-shtikh*

My tongue is coated – Meine Zunge ist belegt
mine**-è **tsoong**-è ist bè-**laygt

My stomach is upset – Ich habe mir den Magen verdorben
*ikh **hah**-bè meer dayn **mah**-gèn fer-**dor**-bèn*

I feel nauseous – Mir ist übel
*meer ist **o͞o**-bèl*

I think I have food poisoning – Ich glaube, ich habe eine Lebensmittelvergiftung
*ikh **glow**-bè ikh **hah**-bè **ine**-è **lay**-bènz-mi-tèl-fer-**gif**-toong*

I have been sick – Ich habe mich übergeben
*ikh **hah**-bè mikh o͞o-ber-**gay**-bèn*

I have diarrhoea – Ich habe Durchfall
*ikh **hah**-bè **doorkh**-fal*

I am constipated – Ich habe Verstopfung
*ikh **hah**-bè fer-**shtop**-foong*

I feel faint – Ich fühle mich schwach
*ikh **fo͞o**-lè mikh shvakh*

I feel dizzy – Mir ist schwindelig
*meer ist **shvin**-dè-likh*

The Doctor
Conditions

I am allergic to penicillin – Ich reagiere allergisch auf Penizillin
*ikh ray-a-**gee**-rè a-**ler**-gish owf pen-i-tsi-**leen***

I have high blood pressure – Ich habe zu hohen Blutdruck
*ikh **hah**-bè tsoo **hō**-èn **bloot**-drook*

I am a diabetic – Ich bin zuckerkrank
*ikh bin **tsoo**-kèr-krank*

I am taking these drugs – Ich nehme diese Medikamente
*ikh **nay**-mè **dee**-zè me-di-ka-**men**-tè*

Can you give me a German prescription for them? – Können Sie mir dafür ein deutsches Rezept geben?
*__kur'n__-èn zee meer **dah**-fōōr ine **doyt**-shès re-**tsept** **gay**-bèn?*

I am pregnant – Ich bin schwanger
*ikh bin **shvang**-èr*

I am on the pill – Ich nehme die Pille
*ikh **nay**-mè dee **pil**-è*

My blood group is . . . – Ich habe die Blutgruppe . . .
*ikh **hah**-bè dee **bloot**-groo-pè . . .*

I don't know my blood group – Ich weiß nicht, welche Blutgruppe ich habe
*ikh vice nikht **vel**-khè **bloot**-groo-pè ikh **hah**-bè*

Must I stay in bed? – Muß ich im Bett bleiben?
*mooss ikh im bet **blye**-bèn?*

Will I be able to go out tomorrow? – Darf ich morgen ausgehen?
*darf ikh **mor**-gèn **ows**-gay-èn?*

How soon can I travel? – Wann kann ich wieder reisen?
*van kan ikh **vee**-dèr **rye**-zèn?*

Will I have to go into hospital? – Muß ich ins Krankenhaus?
*mooss ikh ins **krang**-kèn-hows?*

Will an operation be necessary? – Muß operiert werden?
*mooss opè-**ree**-yert **ver**-dèn?*

The Doctor
Parts of the Body

Here is my E111 form – Hier ist mein internationaler Krankenschein
*heer ist mine in-ter-nat-see-ō-**nah**-ler **krang**-kèn-shine*

How do I get reimbursed? – Wie werden mir die Kosten zurückerstattet?
*vee **ver**-dèn meer dee **kos**-tèn zoo-**rook**-er-shta-tèt?*

ankle Knöchel *knur'kh-èl*
arm Arm *arm*
back Rücken ***roo**-ken*
bone Knochen ***kno**-khèn*
breast Brust *broost*
cheek Wange ***vang**-è*
chest Brustkorb ***broost**-korp*
ear Ohr *or*
elbow Ellbogen ***el**-bō-gèn*
eye Auge ***ow**-gè*
face Gesicht *gè-**zikht***
finger Finger ***fing**-er*
foot Fuß *fooss*
hand Hand *hant*
heart Herz *herts*
kidney Niere ***nee**-rè*
knee Knie *kè-**nee***
leg Bein *bine*
liver Leber ***lay**-bèr*
lungs Lungen ***loong**-èn*
mouth Mund *moont*
muscle Muskel ***moos**-kèl*
neck Hals *hals*
nose Nase ***nah**-zè*
shin Schienbein ***sheen**-bine*
skin Haut *howt*
spine Wirbelsäule ***veer**-bèl-zoy-lè*
stomach Magen ***mah**-gèn*
throat Hals *hals*
tonsils Mandeln ***man**-dèln*
wrist Handgelenk ***hant**-gè-lenk*

The Dentist

I need to see the dentist – Ich muß zum Zahnartz
*ikh mooss tsoom **tsahn**-artst*

I have a toothache – Ich habe Zahnschmerzen
*ikh **hah**-bè **tsahn**-shmerts-èn*

It's this one – Es ist dieser Zahn
*es ist **dee**-zèr tsahn*

I've broken a tooth – Mir ist ein Zahn abgebrochen
*meer ist ine tsahn **ap**-gè-brokh-èn*

The filling has come out – Die Plombe ist herausgefallen
*dee **plom**-bè ist he-**rows**-gè-fal-èn*

Will you have to take it out? – Müssen Sie ihn ziehen?
***mōōss**-èn zee een **tsee**-èn?*

Are you going to fill it? – Werden Sie ihn plombieren?
***ver**-dèn zee een plom-**bee**-rèn?*

That hurts – Das tut weh
dass toot vay

Please give me an injection – Bitte geben Sie mir eine Spritze
***bit**-è **gay**-bèn zee meer **ine**-è **shprit**-sè*

My gums hurt – Das Zahnfleisch tut mir weh
*dass **tsahn**-flye-sh toot meer vay*

My false teeth are broken – Mein Gebiß ist kaputt
*mine gè-**biss** ist ka-**poot***

Can you repair them? – Können Sie es reparieren?
***kur'n**-èn zee es re-pa-**ree**-rèn?*

The Time

What time is it? –	Wieviel Uhr ist es? ***vee**-feel **oo**-èr ist es?*	
It is . . . –	Es ist . . . *es ist . . .*	
10 o'clock –	zehn Uhr *tsayn **oo**-èr*	
5 past 10	fünf *fōōnf*	nach zehn *nahkh tsayn*
10 past 10	zehn *tsayn*	
a quarter past 10	viertel ***feer**-tèl*	
20 past 10	zwanzig ***tsvan**-tsikh*	
25 past 10	fünfundzwanzig ***fōōnf**-oont-tsvan-tsikh*	
half past 10 –	halb elf *halp elf*	
25 to 11	fünfundzwanzig ***fōōnf**-oont-tsvan-tsikh*	vor elf *for elf*
20 to 11	zwanzig ***tsvan**-tsikh*	
a quarter to 11	viertel ***feer**-tèl*	
10 to 11	zehn *tsayn*	
5 to 11	fünf *fōōnf*	
11 o'clock –	elf Uhr *elf **oo**-èr*	
12 o'clock (midday) –	zwölf Uhr mittags *tsvur'lf **oo**-èr **mi**-tahks*	
(midnight) –	zwölf Uhr nachts *tsvur'lf **oo**-èr nakhts*	

The Time

A few of these expressions may be useful:

tonight – heute abend
***hoy**-tè **ah**-bènt*

at night – nachts
nakhts

the morning – der Morgen
*der **mor**-gèn*

this afternoon – heute nachmittag
***hoy**-tè **nahkh**-mi-tahk*

before midnight – vor Mitternacht
*for **mi**-ter-nakht*

after 3 o'clock – nach drei Uhr
*nahkh drye **oo**-èr*

at half past six – um halb sieben
*oom halp **zee**-bèn*

nearly 5 o'clock – kurz vor fünf
koorts for fo͞onf

at about 1 o'clock – gegen ein Uhr
***gay**-gèn **ine oo**-èr*

in an hour's time – in einer Stunde
*in **ine**-èr **shtoon**-dè*

two hours ago – vor zwei Stunden
*for tsvye **shtoon**-dèn*

in half an hour – in einer halben Stunde
*in **ine**-èr **hal**-bèn **shtoon**-dè*

soon – bald
balt

early – früh
fro͞o

late – spät
shpayt

Numbers
Up to a million

0	null *nool*	21	einundzwanzig ***ine**-oont-tsvan-tsikh*
1	eins *ines*	22	zweiundzwanzig ***tsvye**-oont-tsvan-tsikh*
2	zwei *tsvye*	23	dreiundzwanzig ***drye**-oont-tsvan-tsikh*
3	drei *drye*	30	dreißig ***drye**-sikh*
4	vier *feer*	40	vierzig ***feer**-tsikh*
5	fünf *fōōnf*	50	fünfzig ***fōōnf**-tsikh*
6	sechs *zekhs*	60	sechzig ***zekh**-tsikh*
7	sieben ***zee**-bèn*	70	siebzig ***zeep**-tsikh*
8	acht *akht*	80	achtzig ***akh**-tsikh*
9	neun *noyn*	90	neunzig ***noyn**-tsikh*
10	zehn *tsayn*	100	hundert ***hoon**-dert*
11	elf *elf*	101	hunderteins ***hoon**-dert-ines*
12	zwölf *tsvur'lf*	110	hundertzehn ***hoon**-dert-tsayn*
13	dreizehn ***drye**-tsayn*	200	zweihundert ***tsvye**-hoon-dert*
14	vierzehn ***feer**-tsayn*	300	dreihundert ***drye**-hoon-dert*
15	fünfzehn ***fōōnf**-tsayn*	400	vierhundert ***veer**-hoon-dert*
16	sechzehn ***zekh**-tsayn*	500	fünfhundert ***fōōnf**-hoon-dert*
17	siebzehn ***zeep**-tsayn*	1,000	tausend ***tow**-zènt*
18	achtzehn ***akh**-tsayn*	2,000	zweitausend ***tsvye**-tow-zènt*
19	neunzehn ***noyn**-tsayn*	5,000	fünftausend ***fōōnf**-tow-zènt*
20	zwanzig ***tsvan**-tsikh*	1,000,000	eine Million ***ine**-è mi-lee-ōn*

Numbers
The First to the Last

1st	erste ***erst***-*è*	**16th**	sechszehnte ***zekh***-*tsayn-tè*
2nd	zweite ***tsvye***-*tè*	**17th**	siebzehnte ***zeep***-*tsayn-tè*
3rd	dritte ***dri***-*tè*	**18th**	achtzehnte ***akh***-*tsayn-tè*
4th	vierte ***feer***-*tè*	**19th**	neunzehnte ***noyn***-*tsayn-tè*
5th	fünfte ***fōōnf***-*tè*	**20th**	zwanzigste ***tsvan***-*tsikh-stè*
6th	sechste ***zekhs***-*tè*	**21st**	einundzwanzigste ***ine***-*oont-tsvan-tsikh-stè*
7th	siebte ***zeep***-*tè*	**22nd**	zweiundzwanzigste ***tsvye***-*oont-tsvan-zikh-stè*
8th	achte ***akh***-*tè*	**23rd**	dreiundzwanzigste ***dry***-*oont-tsvan-tsikh-stè*
9th	neunte ***noyn***-*tè*	**30th**	dreißigste ***drye***-*sikh-stè*
10th	zehnte ***tsayn***-*tè*	**40th**	vierzigste ***feer***-*tsikh-stè*
11th	elfte ***elf***-*tè*	**50th**	fünfzigste ***fōōnf***-*tsikh-stè*
12th	zwölfte ***tsvur'lf***-*tè*	**100th**	hundertste ***hoon***-*dert-stè*
13th	dreizehnte ***drye***-*tsayn-tè*	**1,000th**	tausendste ***tow***-*zènt-stè*
14th	vierzehnte ***feer***-*tsayn-tè*		
15th	fünfzehnte ***fōōnf***-*tsayn-tè*		

a half	ein halbes *ine **hal**-bès*	**a dozen**	ein Dutzend *ine **doo**-tsènt*
a quarter	ein Viertel *ine **feer**-tèl*	**half a dozen**	ein halbes Dutzend *ine **hal**-bès **doo**-tsènt*
a third	ein Drittel *ine **dri**-tèl*	**5 times**	fünf mal ***fōōnf** mal*
two thirds	zwei Drittel *tsvye **dri**-tèl*	**the last (one)**	der letzte *der let-stè*
10%	zehn Prozent *tsayn prō-**tsent***		

The Calendar

Sunday	Sonntag ***zon**-tahk*	**January**	Januar ***yan**-oo-ar*
Monday	Montag ***mōn**-tahk*	**February**	Februar ***fay**-broo-ar*
Tuesday	Dienstag ***deens**-tahk*	**March**	März *merts*
Wednesday	Mittwoch ***mit**-vokh*	**April**	April *a-**pril***
Thursday	Donnerstag ***don**-ers-tahk*	**May**	Mai *mye*
Friday	Freitag ***frye**-tahk*	**June**	Juni ***yoo**-nee*
Saturday	Samstag ***zams**-tahk*	**July**	Juli ***yoo**-lee*
on Friday	am Freitag *am **frye**-tahk*	**August**	August *ow-**goost***
next Tuesday	nächsten Dienstag ***naykhs**-tèn **deens**-tahk*	**September**	September *sep-**tem**-bèr*
		October	Oktober *ok-**tō**-bèr*
yesterday	gestern ***ges**-tèrn*	**November**	November *nō-**vem**-bèr*
today	heute ***hoy**-tè*	**December**	Dezember *day-**tsem**-bèr*
tomorrow	morgen ***mor**-gèn*	**in June**	im Juni *im **yoo**-nee*
spring	Frühling ***froo**-ling*	**July 6th**	der sechste Juli *der **zekh**-tè **yoo**-lee*
summer	Sommer ***zom**-èr*	**next week**	nächste Woche ***naykh**-stè **vo**-khè*
autumn (fall)	Herbst *herpst*	**last month**	letzten Monat ***let**-stèn **mō**-nat*
winter	Winter ***vin**-tèr*		
in spring	im Frühling *im **froo**-ling*		
in summer	im Sommer *im **zom**-èr*		

Public Holidays

New Year's Day	January 1st	
Epiphany	January 6th	
Good Friday	(*not Austria*)	
Easter Monday		
Labour Day	May 1st	
Ascension Day		
Whit Monday		
Corpus Christi		
Assumption	August 15th	(*Austria only*)
National Day	October 26th	(*Austria only*)
All Saints' Day	November 1st	
Repentance Day	November 21st	(*not Austria*)
Feast of the Immaculate Conception	December 8th	(*Austria only*)
Christmas Day	December 25th	
St. Stephen's Day	December 26th	

The Alphabet

A	**wie**	**Anton**	**N**	**wie**	**Nordpol**
ah	*vee*	***an**-ton*	*en*	*vee*	***nort**-pōl*
B	for	**Berta**	**O**	for	**Otto**
bay		***ber**-ta*	*ō*		***o**-tō*
C		**Caesar**	**P**		**Paula**
tsay		***tsay**-zar*	*pay*		***pow**-lah*
D		**Dora**	**Q**		**Quelle**
day		***dō**-rah*	*kōō*		***kwe**-lè*
E		**Emil**	**R**		**Richard**
ay		***ay**-meel*	*er*		***rikh**-art*
F		**Friedrich**	**S**		**Siegfried**
ef		***freed**-rikh*	*es*		***zeek**-freet*
G		**Gustav**	**T**		**Theodor**
gay		***goos**-tahf*	*tay*		***tay**-ō-dor*
H		**Heinrich**	**U**		**Ulrich**
hah		***hine**-rikh*	*oo*		***ool**-rikh*
I		**Ida**	**V**		**Victor**
ee		***ee**-dah*	*fow*		***vik**-tor*
J		**Julius**	**W**		**Wilhelm**
yot		***yoo**-lee-oos*	*vay*		***vil**-helm*
K		**Konrad**	**X**		**Xanten**
kah		***kon**-rat*	*iks*		***ksan**-tèn*
L		**Ludwig**	**Y**		
el		***lood**-vikh*	***ōōp**-si-lon*		
M		**Martin**	**Z**		**Zeppelin**
em		***mar**-tin*	*tset*		***tse**-pè-leen*

ä, ö, ü are read as *ah*, *ō*, *oo*, umlaut (***oom**-lowt*)
ß is read as Eszett (***es**-tset*)

Descriptions

First of all, a list of colours:

beige	beige *bayj*	**mauve**	violett *vee-ō-**let***
black	schwarz *shvarts*	**orange**	orange *o-**ran**-jè*
blue	blau *blow*	**pink**	rosa ***rō**-za*
brown	braun *brown*	**purple**	lila ***lee**-la*
cream	creme *kraym*	**red**	rot *rōt*
fawn	hellbraun ***hel**-brown*	**silver**	silber ***zil**-bèr*
gold	gold *golt*	**tan**	gelbbraun ***gelp**-brown*
green	grün *grōōn*	**white**	weiß *vice*
grey	grau *grow*	**yellow**	gelb *gelp*

and a few other handy adjectives:

bad	shlecht *shlekht*	**good**	gut *goot*
beautiful	schön *shur'n*	**high**	hoch *hōkh*
big	groß *grōss*	**hot**	heiß *hice*
cheap	billig ***bil**-ikh*	**little**	klein *kline*
cold	kalt *kalt*	**long**	lang *lang*
dear	teuer ***toy**-èr*	**new**	neu *noy*
difficult	schwierig ***shvee**-rikh*	**old**	alt *alt*
easy	leicht *lye-kht*	**short**	kurz *koorts*
fast	schnell *shnel*	**slow**	langsam ***lang**-zahm*

Conversion Tables

In these tables you can treat the middle figure as either a metric or an imperial measurement. So to convert from pounds to kilos you look at the figure on the right, and for kilos to pounds, you want the figure on the left.

lb		kg
2.2	1	0.45
4.4	2	0.91
6.6	3	1.4
8.8	4	1.8
11	5	2.2
13.2	6	2.7
15.4	7	3.2
17.6	8	3.6
19.8	9	4.1
22	10	4.5

inches		cm
0.39	1	2.54
0.79	2	5.08
1.18	3	7.62
1.57	4	10.6
1.97	5	12.7
2.36	6	15.2
2.76	7	17.8
3.15	8	20.3
3.54	9	22.9
3.9	10	25.4
4.3	11	27.9
4.7	12	30.1

feet		metres
3.3	1	0.3
6.6	2	0.61
9.9	3	0.91
13.1	4	1.22
16.4	5	1.52
19.7	6	1.83
23	7	2.13
26.2	8	2.44
29.5	9	2.74
32.9	10	3.05

Conversion Tables

Kilometres	Miles	Centigrade	Fahrenheit
10	6.2	0	32
20	12.4	5	41
30	18.6	10	50
40	24.9	15	59
50	31	17	63
60	37.3	20	68
70	43.5	22	72
80	49.7	24	75
90	56	26	79
100	62	28	82
110	68.3	30	86
120	74.6	35	95
130	81	37	98.4
140	87	38	100
150	93.2	40	104
160	100	50	122
200	124	100	212
300	186		
500	310		

Exchange Rates

£1 =	$1 =
1 DM =	50 DM =
5 DM =	100 DM =
10 DM =	250 DM =
25 DM =	500 DM =

Place-names

Aachen	***ah**-khèn*
Admont	***at**-mont*
Ansbach	***ans**-bakh*
Augsburg	***owks**-boork*
Badgastein	*bahd-gas-**tine***
Bad Ischl	*bahd **ish**-èl*
Baden	***bah**-dèn*
Bad Reichenhall	*bahd **rye**-khèn-hal*
Bad Wimpfen	*bahd **vimp**-fèn*
Baden-Baden	***bah**-dèn **bah**-dèn*
Bamberg	***bam**-berk*
Bayreuth	*bye-**royt***
Berchtesgaden	***berkh**-tès-gah-dèn*
Bernkastel	*bern-**kas**-tèl*
Berlin	*ber-**leen***
Bielefeld	***bee**-lè-felt*
Bingen	***bing**-èn*
Bludenz	***bloo**-dents*
Bonn	*bon*
Börstingen	***bur'**-sting-èn*
Braunschweig (Brunswick)	***brown**-shvike*
Bregenz	***bray**-gents*
Bremen	***bray**-mèn*
Bremerhaven	***bray**-mèr-hah-fèn*
Celle	***tse**-lè*
Cuxhaven	*kooks-**hah**-fèn*
Darmstadt	***darm**-shtat*
Dinkelsbühl	***ding**-kèlz-bōōl*
Dortmund	***dort**-moont*
Dürnstein	***dōōrn**-shtine*
Düsseldorf	***dōō**-sèl-dorf*
Eisenstadt	***ize**-èn-shtat*
Erbach	***er**-bakh*
Essen	***ess**-èn*
Frankfurt	***frank**-foort*
Frauenchiemsee	***frow**-èn-**keem**-zay*
Freiburg	***frye**-boork*
Freudenstadt	***froy**-dèn-shtat*
Fulda	***fool**-dah*
Füssen	***fōō**-sèn*
Garmisch-Partenkirchen	***gar**-mish-**par**-tèn-**keer**-khèn*
Graz	*grahts*
Halle	***ha**-lè*
Hallstadt	***hal**-shtat*
Hamburg	***ham**-boork*
Hameln	***hahm**-èln*
Hannover	*ha-**nō**-fèr*
Heidelberg	***hye**-dèl-berk*
Heilbronn	*hile-**bron***
Heiligenkreuz	***hye**-lig-èn-kroyts*
Herrenchiemsee	***he**-rèn-**keem**-zay*
Hinterzarten	***hin**-tèr-tsar-tèn*
Hornberg	***horn**-berk*

Place-names

Innsbruck	***ins**-brook*
Jagsthausen	***jahkst**-how-zèn*
Karlsruhe	***karls**-roo-è*
Kassel	***kass**-èl*
Kiel	*keel*
Kitzbühel	***kits**-bōōl*
Klagenfurt	***klah**-gèn-foort*
Koblenz	***kō**-blents*
Konstanz	***kon**-stants*
Köln (Cologne)	*kur'ln*
Landau	***lan**-dow*
Landshut	***lants**-hoot*
Leipzig	***lipe**-tsikh*
Limburg	***lim**-boork*
Lindau	***lin**-dow*
Linz	*lints*
Lübeck	***lōō**-bek*
Magdeburg	***mak**-dè-boork*
Mainz	*myents*
Mannheim	***man**-hime*
Mariazell	*ma-ree-a-**tsel***
Maulbronn	*mowl-**bron***
Meersburg	***may**-èrz-boork*
Melk	*melk*
Mittenwald	***mi**-tèn-valt*
München (Munich)	***mōōn**-khèn*
Münster	***mōōn**-stèr*
Nürnberg (Nuremberg)	***nōōrn**-berk*
Oberammergau	*ō-bèr-**am**-er-gow*
Oberstorf	***ō**-berst-dorf*
Neuss	*noys*
Passau	***pass**-ow*
Potsdam	***pots**-dam*
Rattenberg	***ra**-tèn-berk*
Regensburg	***ray**-gènz-boork*
Rostock	***ros**-tok*
Rothenburg	***rō**-tèn-boork*
Rüdesheim	***rōō**-des-hime*
Salzburg	***zalts**-boork*
Schwäbisch-Hall	*shvay-bish-**hal***
Schwetzingen	***shvet**-tsing-èn*
Stuttgart	***shtoot**-gart*
Travemünde	*tra-vè-**mōōn**-dè*
Triberg	***tree**-berk*
Trier	*treer*
Tübingen	***tōō**-bing-èn*
Ulm	*oolm*
Wien (Vienna)	*veen*
Wiesbaden	***vees**-bah-dèn*
Wuppertal	***voo**-pèr-tahl*
Würzburg	***vōōrts**-boork*

Signs & Notices

Achtung –	Caution
Aufzug –	Lift/elevator
Ausgang –	Exit
Auskunft –	Information
Äußerlich zu gebrauchen –	For external use only
Ausverkauf –	Sale
Ausverkauft –	Sold out
Besetzt –	Occupied
Betreten des Rasens verboten –	Keep off the grass
Bitte klingeln –	Please ring
Das Sprechen mit dem Fahrer während der Fahrt ist verboten –	It is forbidden to speak to the driver while the bus is moving
Drücken –	Push
Eingang –	Entrance
Eintreten ohne zu klopfen –	Enter without knocking
Eintritt frei –	No admission charge
Fernsprecher –	Telephone
Feuerwehr –	Fire Brigade
Frei –	Vacant
Fundbüro –	Lost Property Office
Für Unbefugte verboten –	No trespassing
Gefahr –	Danger
Geschlossen –	Closed
Gift –	Poison
Heiß –	Hot
Hinten einsteigen –	Enter at the rear (*on trams*)
Kalt –	Cold
Kasse –	Pay here
Kein Durchgang –	No thoroughfare
Kein Zutritt –	No entrance

Signs & Notices

Krankenhaus – Hospital
Krankenwagen – Ambulance
Lebensgefahr – Danger of death
Nachmittags geschlossen – Closed in the afternoon
Nicht berühren – Do not touch
Nicht hinauslehnen – Do not lean out
Nichtraucher – No smoking
Notausgang – Emergency Exit
Notbremse – Communication cord
Nur für Anlieger – Parking for residents only
Privatweg – Private road
Radweg – Cycle path
Rauchen verboten – No smoking
Raucher – Smokers' compartment
Räumungsverkauf – Closing down sale
Rechts fahren – Keep to the right
Reiseandenken – Souvenirs
Reisebüro – Travel Agency
Schlußverkauf – Sale
Sonderangebot – Special offer
Toilette während des Aufenthalts in Bahnhöfen nicht benutzen – Do not use toilet while train is in station
Trinkwasser – Drinking water
Umleitung – Diversion
Unbefugtes Betreten verboten – No trespassing
. . . verboten – . . . forbidden
Vorsicht – Caution
Ziehen – Pull
Zu verkaufen – For sale
Zu vermieten – To let/For hire

Index

Index

Index

Index

Index

Personal Details

Name ....
Name
Home address ....
Heimatadresse

....

....

Tel ....

Address in Germany ....
Adresse in Deutschland

....

....

Tel ....

In case of accident notify ....
Bei Unfall bitte Mitteilung an

....

....

....

Tel ....

Passport No. ....
Reisepaß Nr
Car No. ....
Kfz-Kennzeichen
Blood group ....
Blutgruppe

HALT sign — All Vehicles Prohibited — STOP Customs — No Parking I on even days II on odd days — Use of Horn Prohibited — Speed Limit

DANGER — Tunnel — Loose Chippings — Slippery Road — Cross Roads with minor road — Cross Winds

PRIORITY ROAD — END of priority. Give way to traffic from right. — DANGER Give way to traffic from right. (France) — PRIORITY ROAD. — Level Crossing

Minimum Speed Limit — END of Minimum Speed — Keep Right — Switch on headlights — Snow Chains or Tyres Compulsory — Cycle path Compulsory

First Aid — First Aid — Information — Subway or Bridge — Pedestrian Crossing — Mechanical Help — Filling Station